basic
MULTITRACKING

Design: David Houghton

Printed by: MPG Books, Bodmin

Published by: Sanctuary Publishing Limited, Sanctuary House, 45-53 Sinclair Road, London W14 0NS, United Kingdom. Web site: www.sanctuarypublishing.com

Copyright: Paul White, 1999
Sound On Sound web site: www.sospubs.co.uk

ISBN: 1-86074-264-5

Also by Paul White from Sanctuary Publishing

Creative Recording I – Effects & Processors
Creative Recording II – Microphones, Acoustics,
    Soundproofing & Monitoring
Home Recording Made Easy
MIDI For The Technophobe
Live Sound For The Performing Musician
Recording & Production Techniques
Music Technology – A Survivor's Guide

Also in this series

basic DIGITAL RECORDING
basic EFFECTS AND PROCESSORS
basic HOME STUDIO DESIGN
basic LIVE SOUND
basic MASTERING
basic MICROPHONES
basic MIDI
basic MIXERS
basic MIXING TECHNIQUES

basic
MULTITRACKING

PAUL WHITE

contents

chapter 2

chapter 3

chapter 4

chapter 5

RECORDING AND MIXING **145**

introduction

Affordable multitrack recording enables anyone with basic musical skills and ideas to record and mix their own compositions at home using their own equipment. The other major revolutions in music making are MIDI and sequencing, which are covered more fully in the *basic MIDI* book that is a part of this series. The technology may be affordable, yet the quality of the end result can rival the output from professional studio, providing you know how to get the best out of your equipment.

Originally multitrack recording meant recording onto analogue tape, but now we have the choice of analogue or digital tape, and tapeless recording using either dedicated hard disk recorders or computers. Fortunately, even computer-based systems emulate the analogue tape-based environment to some extent, so if you know how multitracking works with tape, you should have no trouble transferring your skills to the tapeless domain. The first section of this book describes traditional tape-based methods of working, then goes on to discuss digital tape as well as tapeless systems.

You don't have to be a technical whizz to use recording equipment any more than you need to know all about photography to use an automatic camera, but as with all practical subjects, there are right ways and wrong ways to do things. The author has had many years experience in recording and has stripped away much of the jargon and mystery that surrounds the subject to explain the whole recording process in a straightforward, non-technical way.

You can only fully master recording by actually doing it, which is why this book takes a very practical approach, comprehensively illustrated with easy-to-follow diagrams. No matter whether you are working with a simple cassette deck and two mics, or a full multitrack recording studio, this book will help you produce more professional results. Over two decades of experience are concentrated in these pages, making *basic MULTITRACKING* one of the most useful studio accessories you'll ever own.

basic concepts

While it is possible to record music onto analogue tape, digital tape, hard disk or removable magnetic and magneto-optical computer media, analogue-tape-based systems are still the easiest to understand. The simplest of these are the cassette multitrackers, which usually provide four tracks of recording capability. To explain the basics of multitrack recording it's probably best to start with the old analogue tape model, even if your ultimate aim is to use a digital tapeless system.

The key point of multitrack recording is that it enables musical compositions to be built up in layers and removes the need to have everything played, mixed and recorded at the same time. Clearly this makes it particularly attractive for solo musicians working at home who may want to play and sing many or all of the musical parts themselves.

A conventional analogue tape machine, such as a cassette deck, employs a record head, which converts the incoming music waveform into an alternating magnetic field. This field is the medium by which magnetic information is transferred from the head onto the magnetic tape. When the tape is played back, the magnetic message, now stored on the tape, is read by a playback head and then amplified to reproduce the original electrical signal.

tape tracks

Magnetic tape comprises a flexible strip of durable, non-magnetic material coated with a layer of specially-formulated oxide particles designed to retain magnetic information. The simplest form of recorder is the single-track or mono machine, which records the magnetic information as a single invisible stripe along the length of the tape.

Because the tape is designed to be re-usable, an erase head is positioned just in front of the record head so that, when a recording is made, the erase head wipes the tape just before it arrives at the record head. If you think of the magnetic recording as being the magnetic equivalent of a picture drawn in sand, the erase head effectively shakes the sand by applying a high-frequency magnetic field to the tape. To put it another way, the erase process randomises the magnetic information stored on the tape, thus removing any recognisable signal that may once have been present there.

Stereo recorders actually make two different recordings, side by side along the tape, in the form of two parallel tracks. One track feeds the left-hand loudspeaker of a stereo system and the other feeds the right-hand speaker. A stereo record head is really just a combination of two heads: one to record the left-hand signal and one to record the right. Similarly, the playback head is also two heads in one.

audio cassettes

A compact cassette is turned over once it reaches the end, which means that more music can be recorded 'on the other side'. Contrary to popular belief this isn't actually recorded on the other side of the tape. What really happens is that the two recordings exist on the same side of the tape but they run in opposite directions, like lanes on a two-lane highway. Side one is represented by two lanes running in one direction and side two by the two lanes running in the other direction, as shown in Figure 1.1.

The figure also shows how the tracks are arranged in

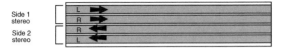

Side 1
stereo

Side 2
stereo

Figure 1.1a: Track layout of a conventional stereo cassette

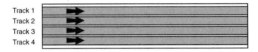

Track 1
Track 2
Track 3
Track 4

Figure 1.1b: Track layout of a cassette multitracker

a four-track multitrack recorder. Note that the track layout is the same with the exception that now all four tracks are being recorded in the same direction and are all played back at the same time. This means that the tape can't be turned over – it can only be used in one direction. It's also important to understand that there is no difference between a mono, stereo or multitrack tape or cassette. Recording tape is a single strip of flexible plastic coated on one side with magnetic material. The tracks themselves are created by the record head in the tape machine. This is why the same brand of quarter-inch tape can be used on mono, stereo, four-track and even eight-track recorders.

multitrack recorders

Multitrack tape machines can record from four to 24 tracks of audio on tape that ranges from a quarter of an inch to two inches wide. Eight tracks is the current maximum for cassette-based systems, with four being more common. These tracks may be recorded all at once, a few at once or independently, depending on the working arrangements, though some cheaper cassette multitrackers restrict recording to no more than two tracks at a time. This is important if you're looking for a machine to record a live band, when you'll need to have all available tracks recording at once.

Using a multitrack recorder you can either record a live performance in one take and then mix it afterwards, or you can build up your composition an instrument at a time. In practice most people record the first few tracks all at once and then add extra instruments and vocals afterwards. This process is known as overdubbing.

The ability to build up a recording in layers offers several advantages. For example, one musician can play or sing many different parts in the same piece of music, and when the recording is finished the levels of the different tracks can be balanced and panned to give the perfect mix. Effects, such as echo or reverb, can be added during the mix. And even when all of the musicians play together, multitrack recording provides the ability to record each instrument and voice separately, allowing the balance and tone of each instrument to be adjusted during the mix.

overdubbing

After the first tracks have been recorded you will need some way of hearing these play back while you overdub new parts. For example, if the band has just played the bass, drums and rhythm guitar parts of a song, you will then need to hear this along with the lead vocal or the guitar solo. Listening to a signal being played back on a tape machine is known as monitoring, and when overdubs are being recorded this is generally done by using headphones to prevent the previously-recorded sound spilling back into the microphone. Unless you have a cassette multitracker, or one of the tapeless equivalents that combines the function of a recorder and a mixer, you'll need a mixer for both recording and monitoring playback when overdubbing.

tape monitoring

On early multitrack machines different heads were used for recording and playback, and this led to timing problems during overdubbing. These problems arose because the record head was a little way further along the tape path than the replay head, resulting in a fraction of a second delay between the recorded and replayed sound.

Complicated switching systems were devised to solve this problem, but all cassette multitrackers and virtually

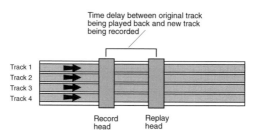

Time delay between original track being played back and new track being recorded

Track 1
Track 2
Track 3
Track 4

Record head

Replay head

Figure 1.2a: Separate record and playback heads

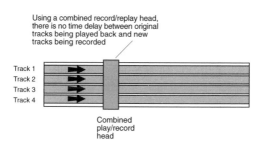

Using a combined record/replay head, there is no time delay between original tracks being played back and new tracks being recorded

Track 1
Track 2
Track 3
Track 4

Combined play/record head

Figure 1.2b: Combined record and playback head

all modern semi-pro open-reel analogue multitrack recorders use the same head for both recording and playback, which neatly avoids the problem. Figure 1.2 shows the delay problem associated with older multitracks and also the simpler modern system, which uses a combined play/record head. Hardware digital recorders don't have this problem at all, which means that you can monitor what's on tape while overdubbing and be confident that everything will be in sync.

latency

While hardware tapeless recorders tend to take care of monitoring sync for you, a number of low-cost, computer-based recording systems suffer from what is known as monitoring latency. This means that, as overdubbing occurs, the part that is actually sung or played is delayed before it reaches the headphones. This is because it has to pass through the computer's processing chain before it can be monitored. Monitoring latency can really throw your timing so it's often best to use the mixer to monitor the signal being recorded directly rather than rely on the monitoring program built into the software you're using.

A single tape track can be used to record only a mono signal, so an eight-track recorder gives you eight mono tracks. Stereo signals, such as the output from a stereo drum machine or keyboard, need to be recorded onto two tracks, which must then be panned right and left in the mix to recreate the original stereo image. In many instances, however, signals are recorded in mono and then positioned across the soundstage during the mix by using the mixer's pan controls. For example, there's little point in recording a lead vocal in stereo as it's possible to use the mixer pan control to place it anywhere between the left and right speakers.

There are advantages in recording some instruments in true stereo, such as the piano, but the limited number of tracks available on a cassette multitracker makes stereo recording something of a luxury. If you have a system that provides eight tracks or more then recording stereo parts is a more practical proposition.

punch in/punch out

The concept of multitracking involves recording different tracks at different times and then mixing these tracks to stereo so that the result can be recorded onto a conventional stereo tape machine. Few people make flawless recordings, however, so before mixing it's necessary to fix any mistakes or wrong notes that have been recorded. The important process by which small parts of a recording are replaced with new sections is known as punching in.

Imagine you've recorded a vocal part on track one but one word turns out to be sung flat. You don't have to sing the whole song again, though; you simply start the tape a few seconds before the mistake, sing along with what's already recorded and then, at the right moment, put the machine into record (just on the vocal track!) without stopping the tape. At the end of the new section, ideally between words or phrases, punch out of record again and you will have completed your repair.

Punching in is very simple, but it's important to punch in and out during a slight pause or the repair won't necessarily be seamless. Why should this be? With an analogue recorder there's always a slight overlap in the old and newly-recorded material at the punch-in point because of the physical distance between the erase and record heads. When you punch in the erase head will be switched on, but the short section of tape between the two heads still contains previously-recorded material that has escaped erasure. Consequently, as new material is recorded, it will overlap the old material by the time it takes the tape to move from the erase head to the record head.

When you punch out there will be a slight gap as the short section of tape between the erase head and the record head will already have been erased and nothing new recorded onto it. This might only last a quarter of a second or less, but if it happens in the middle of a sound rather than during a pause you'll almost certainly be able to hear it. Once again, digital systems are often capable of making seamless edits, but it's still best to punch in and out during pauses or the material on each side of your edit may not match up perfectly.

So how is a punch in performed? Most multitrack machines allow you to punch in by first setting the track or tracks in question into Record Ready mode by using the individual track Record Ready buttons. The punch in is then executed by putting the machine into play and then holding down the Play button while pushing down the Record button at the punch-in point. You can punch out again by hitting Stop or, sometimes, Play. Check the manual that came with your recorder to determine the precise procedure you need to follow.

Another system that works with some analogue recorders is to put the machine into record with no tracks selected as 'ready' and then use the Record Ready buttons to drop in and out. Some recorders also let you use a footswitch for punching in and out, which is perfect for musicians working on their own. It's worth consulting your multitrack manual – if there's more than one way to handle a punch in and out, decide which one suits your method of working.

auto monitoring

Before the punch in the existing recording should be monitored, preferably via headphones, which will allow you to sing or play along to get the feel of the piece. When you punch into record, what you hear in the headphones automatically changes from what was originally recorded on the track to the new part that you're now recording, and when you punch out again the monitoring reverts to playing the recording from the tape. Any tracks not set to Record Ready will continue to play normally during a punch in.

Because most tape machines and tapeless recording systems can handle the monitor switching automatically, when you punch in or out the right material is always sent to the headphones, which means that you can concentrate on your performance rather than be distracted by technicalities.

When recording pop music it sometimes helps to make punch in and punch out points coincide with a drum beat in order to hide any slight discontinuity which may occur at the edit points if there are no completely quiet pauses in which to edit. Even if you find suitable gaps in which to punch in and out, you might find that the sustain of an instrument is still audible at the edit points, and, without a beat to disguise it, there's a chance that you might still hear this on the edit. Similarly, its important to start playing before the punch-in point because the act of punching in may record over the sustain of a note that was playing beforehand. Playing the same notes as the original part before the punch-in point will duplicate any sustained notes, which will make the edit less obvious.

bouncing

Having four or even eight tracks on which to record seems wonderful at first, but very soon you'll find that you want to record more parts than you have tracks. There is a way around this: a process called bouncing, which involves mixing together two or more already-recorded tracks and re-recording the result onto a spare track. This applies to digital recorders as well as analogue varieties. If you're working with four tracks, there is a limit to what you can accomplish in one go. It's usually only possible to record three tracks and then bounce them onto the fourth, leaving the first three free to be used for new recordings. This process is shown in Figure 1.3.

It's vitally important to check the quality of a bounced mix because once the original tracks have been wiped there's no going back. Unfortunately there'll always be a slight loss in quality whenever tracks are bounced, but if you set your recording levels with care this can be kept to a minimum.

If you need to really stretch the capacity of your recorder, most multitrack machines will allow you to add one part live as you're bouncing, which means that,

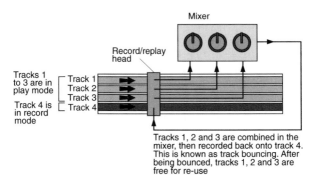

Tracks 1, 2 and 3 are combined in the mixer, then recorded back onto track 4. This is known as track bouncing. After being bounced, tracks 1, 2 and 3 are free for re-use

Figure 1.3: Bouncing tracks

for example, you could play a synth part live while bouncing your drum machine, rhythm guitar and bass parts onto a single track, giving you a total of four parts on one track. If you happen to be working with other musicians you can still record two or more parts at once on the same track but you won't be able to change the balance of these two parts afterwards.

ten-track bounce

Using a simple four-track machine and adding one live part every time a bounce is performed means that a solo musician can record ten different parts onto tape without ever having bounced any sound more than once. The ten-track bounce is achieved thus:

- Record tracks one, two and three.

- Bounce tracks one, two and three to track four while adding a new live part. If you make a mistake recording the live part, you'll have to go back to the start. You can't punch in successfully while working this way, so choose an easy part to play live.

- Check that track four sounds exactly the way you want it to be – you're about to burn your bridges behind you.

- Record new parts over tracks one and two and then bounce these to track three, again adding another new live part as you go.

- Check the result.

- Record over track one and bounce to track two while adding another live part.

- Check the result.

- Finally, record the last part back over track one. Now you're ready to mix.

limitations of bouncing

When you bounce two or more tracks together you are actually making a copy of your original recording onto a new tape track, and of course every time you copy a recording you lose a little sound quality – the noise level increases, and the overall clarity also tends to suffer. Even with a good machine, if you bounce more than once you should expect a drop in sound quality. The best quality will be maintained if you record at the optimum level, and you should always use the meters on the recorder to help you get it right. I'll be discussing levels in greater detail later in the book –

poor level matching is responsible for most of the problems involving sound quality in home recording.

If you're using a standard four-track machine you won't have enough tracks to bounce everything in stereo, so you usually end up with four separate mono submixes on the four tracks, which you will have to pan in the final mix the as well as possible. A little forward planning can be a good investment in making the best of this limitation, and a useful tip is to try and keep all bass and rhythm sounds together so that they can be panned to the centre of the mix. Solos, sound effects and backing vocals can then be panned to other places in the mix to create the illusion of a wide stereo recording. Stereo effects help enormously in this situation, as will be explained later.

what to bounce?

It's a fact that, when recording using analogue tape, some sounds respond more kindly to being bounced than others, and it's also true that a sound that will eventually end up right in the background can usually be bounced without compromising the final product. In contrast, bouncing a lead part destined to be high in the mix will expose any weaknesses. Bright or percussive sounds tend to suffer the most from bouncing, so try not to bounce the drums or lead vocal parts if at all possible.

After gaining a little experience with your machine you'll probably become familiar with the way sounds change when bounced, and you may be able to compensate for this to some extent by adding a little high EQ as you bounce to make up for the drop in brightness that analogue bouncing invariably entails.

recording levels

I mentioned earlier that recording levels are vitally important – if you record at too low a level, your recording will be noisier, with more hiss than it should have, whereas if you record at too high a level the sound will become distorted as the magnetic coating on the tape becomes saturated. Check the meters on your tape machine when recording and then make a test recording to make sure that everything sounds OK. For most material the level meters should go just a little way into the red on the loudest parts of the music, but the absolute level varies from one machine to another and from one brand of tape to another.

Note that, while analogue tape is invariably recorded with peaks pushing the meters up into the red, digital recordings are rather different. There is no safety margin and so it's vital to ensure that signals are as high as they can be without causing the peak or clip indicators to light. Though you might just get away with the odd loud drum beat peaking, digital clipping generally sounds very unpleasant and is to be avoided.

You'll also find that some types of sound show up analogue tape distortion more than other. Vocals and overdrive-style electric guitar can generally be recorded fairly hot before you hear any distortion, while predominantly high-frequency sounds like bells or cymbals, may distort well before the meters go into the red. For this reason, it's very important to make a few test recordings to see how individual machines cope with different types of sound. Ultimately, all that matters is the sound, so listen first and then, if the result is OK, make a note of the meter readings for future reference. I know that keeping a notebook isn't very trendy, but unless you have a perfect memory it's the best way to keep a record of your settings. Again, digital machines don't treat sound the same way, so all you need to do is keep the levels high without allowing the recorder to clip.

trust the meters?

Short or peaky sounds, such as drums, often produce misleading meter readings on mechanical VU meters because the meter mechanism isn't fast enough to respond accurately to very short sounds. In fact, a mechanical VU meter really shows the average sound level as it is perceived by the human ear. With experience it's possible to associate meter readings to various types of sound. These days most machines use bar-graph meters, which are less likely to be misinterpreted as they are are faster and so more accurately represent the peak signal level. However, you will still need to run some tests to find the best levels. Of course your setting may change if you use a different brand of tape, so it's best to find a good brand and then stick with it. Most cassette multitrack recorders are designed to use Type II or chrome-type tape, and it is a false economy to use anything less than the best quality tape.

tape speed

You may have noticed that some cassette multitrack machines run at the same speed as a hi-fi cassette deck whereas others run at twice the speed. As a general rule, the faster the tape speed the lower the tape noise and the better the high-frequency response, so you can expect better recordings from a double speed machine. The down side is that recording time is cut in half. Because multitrack work only uses the tape in one direction, a C60 will last for 30 minutes at normal speed or 15 minutes at double speed. A good tip is to avoid recording anything on the first or last 15 seconds of the tape. If there's a problem with the tape winding unevenly onto the hub, this is where it's most likely to cause audible problems.

varispeed

Multitrack tape recorders are usually fitted with a variable tape speed control known either as varispeed or pitch. This control has a range of only a few percent, but this is enough to push the pitch of a recording up or down by more than a semitone, which is very useful if you're trying to overdub a piano or another instrument that isn't tuned to concert pitch. Simply use the varispeed control to tune your existing recording to the piano, record the piano part and then take the speed back to normal. Varispeed is also useful for helping out singers who can't quite make the high notes – just slow down the tape a little and try again.

tape noise reduction

Semi-pro analogue tape recorders need to use some form of noise reduction system because without it the level of background tape hiss is likely to become obtrusive during passages where the recording isn't loud enough to mask it. Noise-reduction systems provide an effective means of increasing the available dynamic range by reducing the subjective level of tape hiss during quiet passages.

To understand how systems such as Dolby work, it helps to know a little about what went before. There is a very old (but still valid) technique called pre-emphasis/de-emphasis, which involves applying a high-frequency boost to signals during recording and then applying an equal degree of high-frequency cut during playback. This restores the programme material to its original state, but the top cut reduces the level of any high-frequency hiss caused by the tape itself.

Though basic pre- and de-emphasis is rarely used on its own to counter tape hiss, it illustrates very well that noise reduction comprises two stages: the encoding stage, which is applied during recording, and the decoding stage, in which the exact opposite treatment is applied during playback. If the same noise-reduction system isn't used during both recording and playback, the tonal and dynamic accuracy balance of the programme material will compromised.

Tape machines are factory adjusted for a specific brand and type of tape, and the use of any other brand is likely to result in a difference in level on playback that may upset your noise-reduction system. If you want to use a type of tape not recommended for your machine, set the machine up specifically to accommodate your choice of tape.

It's not vital to know how noise reduction works as long as you appreciate that, if you make a recording with a certain type of noise reduction, you will have to play it back using the same type. It's also important to appreciate that such noise-reduction systems only help reduce tape hiss: they don't have any effect on hiss recorded as part of the original signal. The next section investigates the various noise-reduction systems available.

dbx

The majority of Tascam Portastudios use the dbx system, which provides very high levels of noise reduction by combining HF pre-emphasis with 2:1 compression. On replay, a 1:2 expansion (the opposite of compression) is used along with de-emphasis, resulting in a maximum of 30dB of noise reduction. If noise-reduction systems were judged solely on how much hiss they avoided then dbx would be an outright winner, but in reality all noise-reduction systems cause some side-effects that need to be taken into consideration.

Such a high degree of compression means that the replay signal from the tape machine must match the recorded signal very accurately in terms of both level and frequency response. This is because the compressor/expander system magnifies level errors in such a way that a 2dB error in the tape machine becomes a 4dB error after decoding. In theory this implies that the machines best able to benefit from dbx are those that are so good that they don't need it.

To get around this shortcoming, there are actually two different dbx formats; Type 1, for professional use, and Type 2, for domestic sound equipment. Type 2 is used in cassette multitrack machines, where the degree of noise reduction is traded off against a greater tolerance to machine and tape errors.

Dbx works by dramatically increasing the level of quiet signals being recorded to tape with a view to overpowering the tape hiss with brute force. The expansion process on replay reverses the processing and returns the signal to normal, but sometimes it is still possible to hear hiss in the presence of low-frequency sounds where there is no top end present to mask the hiss. A solo bass guitar or deep bass synth may be accompanied by noise which decays as the notes decay. There is little that can be done about this, other than optimising recording levels, and perhaps using some EQ when mixing. Fortunately, it is rarely a problem in the context of a complete mix, as long as recordings are made on good-quality tape.

It's also important, when using dbx, that the recording level should not be driven up into the red but should instead peak at around or just below 0VU. If more level is pushed onto the tape then saturation will cause audible decoding errors, resulting in a dull or squashed sound. In any event, dbx is so effective in reducing noise that it's not necessary to push tape to the limit.

Dolby B

Dolby is still the best-known noise-reduction system, with Dolby B the most popular version for use in domestic hi-fi cassette machines. Unlike dbx, Dolby B only comes into action when the signal falls below a certain threshold level, when the signal becomes too quiet to mask the noise. Because hiss is most audible at higher frequencies Dolby B treats high frequencies differently from low frequencies, and as such it has a lot in common with pre-emphasis/de-emphasis. However, the frequency above which boost is applied during recording varies according to the spectral content of the programme material, and because high level signals that are loud enough to mask the tape noise aren't treated at all there are fewer audible side-effects. Only the vulnerable low level signals are subjected to HF boost. Dolby B is quite a well-behaved system, but it can only achieve a modest 10dB of noise reduction.

It is essential that any recorder using Dolby B is calibrated to give an accurate playback level, or the decoding part of the system will come into action at the wrong threshold value. Dolby B is often accused of sounding dull on domestic hi-fi cassette decks, but I suspect that this is largely due to poor machine alignment or a failure to both record and play back using Dolby B.

Dolby C

Fostex use Dolby C noise reduction for the majority of their cassette multitrackers and open-reel machines, although they have also made Dolby B and Dolby S models. Dolby C works in a way similar to that of Dolby B, but it includes anti-saturation circuitry to prevent HF tape saturation when top boost is being applied to already-bright signals. By helping to prevent tape saturation, decoding errors are reduced.

As well as being a more tolerant system than Dolby B, Dolby C provides a greater degree of of noise reduction – about 20dB. Playing a Dolby B-encoded tape back via Dolby C will sound tonally incorrect, but it will at least be listenable.

Dolby A

Dolby A has been around for almost three decades but is only ever used in professional recording machines and so will not be discussed further here. In recent years, Dolby SR has taken over as the preferred noise-reduction system used by professionals.

Dolby SR

Dolby SR is Dolby's flagship noise-reduction system. It was introduced to give the analogue recorder a longer lease of life in the face of competition from digital machines. Up to 25dB of noise reduction is possible, with minimal side effects, but Dolby SR is both technically complicated and costly to buy. Dolby SR attempts to ensure that the maximum possible amount of energy is recorded in all bands of frequency at all time by using ten filters, some with fixed frequency bands and others that change to cover different parts of the spectrum depending on the programme material. Anti-saturation circuits are included to prevent HF tape from overloading.

Dolby SR means that analogue recordings can sound cleaner and more transparent than the best 16-bit digital recordings, and it is also reasonably tolerant of level errors and changes in tape speed. It is largely because of Dolby SR that many professional studios are still running analogue tape machines rather than moving to digital. It is still a widely-held belief that a good analogue machine has a more musical sound than even the best digital recorder. Dolby SR is unlikely ever to find its way into semi-pro recording equipment, especially as few analogue open-reel recorders are still being built, but the newer Dolby S system offers some of the benefits of SR without the high price.

Dolby S

Dolby S is strictly a semi-pro/consumer system, but it is related to Dolby SR, which is why SR was discussed earlier. Even so, it would be wrong to think of Dolby S as a low-cost version of SR because, in most respects, it's more similar to Dolby C, with the addition of some of the SR filter technology from Dolby SR. Dolby S sounds noticeably more natural than either Dolby B or C, but although it is much cheaper than SR it still costs significantly more than Dolby B or C.

If you don't fully understand the technicalities, at least you'll be aware of what noise reduction can do for you. You should also understand that, to benefit from noise reduction, the recording you make has to be both recorded and played back with it switched on. Though all noise reductions introduce side-effects of varying degrees, these are generally minor compared with the level of background hiss that would be present if noise reduction were not used.

notes on tape care

Good-quality recording starts with good-quality tape, but unless that tape is stored carefully it could start to deteriorate and put your precious recordings at risk. This section is as relevant to digital tape as it is to analogue, as both use similar chemical formulae. Tape should be stored in a dust-free environment (a sealed plastic bag is fine), out of direct sunlight and at a steady room temperature. Because it is a magnetic medium, it should also be kept well away from magnetic fields, such as those generated by loudspeakers, VDUs, power supplies and so on. Don't store paper in with the tape as paper disintegrates with time, causing fine dust to coat the tape.

Never leave tapes in the car or close to radiators as direct sunlight and heat can greatly shorten the life of recording tape. Avoid leaving your tape in a damp or dusty atmosphere, and always ensure the tape machine is clean, especially before making important recordings.

gain structure

On an artistic level the concept of gain structure is pretty boring, but it is the key to making the best recordings of which your equipment is capable. Failure to pay attention to this vital subject will seriously compromise the quality of your recordings, and even professional equipment will perform extremely poorly if the rules explained here are not followed carefully.

The human ear can detect sounds ranging in magnitude and frequency, from the dropping of a pin to nearby thunder, but even the very best recording equipment fails to match this dynamic range. In music, these extremes need never be transgressed: our quietest sounds are rather louder than dropping pins, while the loudest sounds fall well short of the power of thunder. This leaves us with a more realistic dynamic range, with which properly-used electronic equipment can cope. Even so, this range includes signal levels varying from just a few microvolts up to around 20 volts.

At the start of any audio chain is the microphone. Once the signal has left this device it is then electronically amplified to bring it up to line level and then passed through a complex chain of circuitry – which may including mixers, equalisers, amplifiers, effects units and routing systems – before it is recorded onto the master tape.

electrical noise

Each piece of analogue circuitry along the way adds a little more noise to the signal, due to the thermally-induced random movement of electrons, although a well-designed circuit need add only a small amount of noise. While real-life sound signals are always changing in level, the level of noise is essentially constant and so it's evident that, if you feed a very low-level audio signal into a circuit, the ratio of the noise to wanted signal is going to be worse than if you feed in a strong signal. Digital systems also produce noise in the form of quantise distortion, and, although the mechanism by which this is introduced is quite different to that of analogue noise, attention to gain structure is equally important.

The obvious way of minimising the percentage of noise added to a signal is making sure that the signal is at as high a level as possible, but unfortunately there is also a limit to how high a signal level can be before it overloads the circuit through which it's passing. A signal overload causes the circuitry to clip the extremes of the incoming waveform, and the result is audible distortion. Figure 1.4 illustrates this effect.

To avoid the twin evils of noise and clipping distortion, it is important to use the highest possible signal level while still allowing a small safety margin so that any unexpected peaks can pass through without being distorted. If you look at the VU meters on an analogue

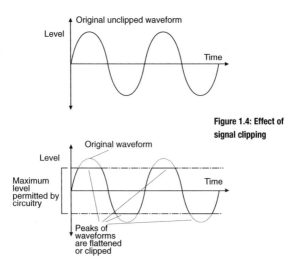

Figure 1.4: Effect of signal clipping

tape recorder you'll see that the optimum operating level is the 0VU mark; the safety headroom is the upper limit to which you can push the level beyond this point before distortion occurs. Figure 1.5 describes a realistic signal level with enough safety margin to accommodate unexpected signal peaks. With digital recorders it's normal to set the peak recording level a little lower than you would with analogue so that unexpected peaks don't cause the recorder to clip.

analogue and digital distortion

Most analogue circuits – and analogue tapes as well, for that matter – don't suddenly clip when the level gets too high; instead the amount of distortion increases progressively until all of the headroom is used up, at which point clipping occurs. This is why the recording-level meters on an analogue tape recorder can occasionally be driven past the 0VU mark up into the red. Distortion increases progressively as the signal level exceeds 0VU, but it's normally possible to go several decibels into the red before the distortion is severe enough to become audible.

Digital circuits and digital tape, on the other hand, have no safety margin or area of progressive distortion beyond 0VU, so clipping occurs immediately . For this reason, the nominal safe operating level for digital equipment is usually around 12dB or so below the 0VU clipping point. Figure 1.6 illustrates how both analogue tape and digital systems response to being overloaded.

Figure 1.5: Headroom to accommodate unexpected signal peaks

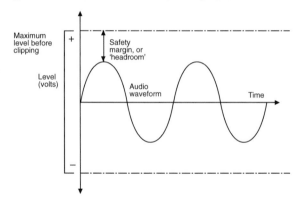

If a signal of insufficient strength is fed into a digital system it is represented by fewer bits, which again results in noise, so just because something is digital it doesn't mean that the old analogue problems don't apply. With both analogue and digital recording it is vital to set the right recording level in order to obtain the best possible sound with the least background noise. The basics of

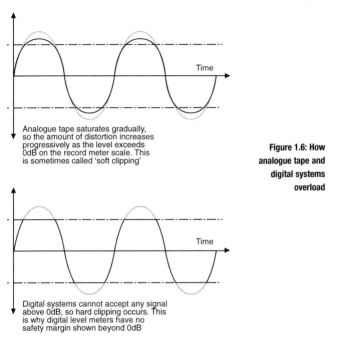

Analogue tape saturates gradually, so the amount of distortion increases progressively as the level exceeds 0dB on the record meter scale. This is sometimes called 'soft clipping'

Figure 1.6: How analogue tape and digital systems overload

Digital systems cannot accept any signal above 0dB, so hard clipping occurs. This is why digital level meters have no safety margin shown beyond 0dB

digital recording are covered later in this book.

gain structure

Put simply, by setting up your gain structure you are ensuring that every piece of circuitry in your studio is running at its optimum signal level – not high enough to cause distortion but also not low enough to allow excessive noise to intrude. This means optimising not only your recording levels but also the levels of any signals fed into your mixer, any signal processing equipment plugged into your mixer and any tape machines fed from your mixer. This sounds more complicated than it actually is. You just have to be methodical when setting up your system, making sure it's properly rigged before you start recording.

Good gain structure starts right back at the microphone pre-amplifier of your mixer, tape deck or cassette multitracker, so if you have a mixer or multitrack workstation equipped with PFL (Pre-Fade Listen) buttons then you can use these to monitor individual inputs. By adjusting the input gain trim controls you can have each signal reading an optimum level on the meters. This takes a few minutes but it's absolutely vital to obtain a good recording. If you're not already familiar with these terms, see the chapter on mixers.

impedance

Electrical resistance is a familiar concept: the higher the resistance the more voltage is needed to force a given current through it. Resistance is measured in ohms, and most people will be familiar with Ohm's law, which states that R = V/I, where V is the voltage across the circuit and I is the current (in amps) flowing through it.

Impedance is essentially a circuit's resistance to an alternating current, such as an audio signal. In a purely resistive circuit resistance and impedance are the same thing, but in a reactive circuit containing capacitors or inductors the impedance will vary in accordance with the frequency of the signal passing through it. Most audio equipment is designed to keep the impedance reasonably constant over the entire audio range, but this isn't always possible in components like loudspeakers.

Input impedance is, in effect, the load that a circuit presents to the device trying to feed the signal into it. But how is output impedance defined? Input impedance is related to the amount of electrical current absorbed by a circuit, whereas output impedance is related to how much current which can be supplied by an output. For one piece of equipment to feed into another without encountering problems, it's important to pay attention to impedance matching.

matching

In electrical terms a matched connection occurs when a circuit with a given output impedance is feeds an input with the same value input impedance. A 600ohm output feeding a 600ohm input would be a perfect match. This is an important factor in any system concerned with transferring the maximum amount of power from one circuit to another. In mechanical terms, impedance matching can be considered to be the electrical equivalent of gear ratios in a car gear box.

With low-level audio signals we're no longer concerned with optimum power transfer: we simply want to send a signal from one place to another without damaging it in any way. To achieve this it's usual for the source impedance (the output impedance of the equipment providing the signal) to be between five and ten times lower than the load impedance (the device accepting the signal). Not only does this prevent the signal from being unduly loaded but it also enables one source to drive multiple loads simultaneously if necessary.

To see how this works in practice, a mixing console has an input impedance of around 1kohm, while a low-impedance dynamic microphone might have an impedance of 200ohms or so. This satisfies the criteria for a good match, as the ratio is 5:1. Line inputs have a typical impedance of 50kohms, while most equipment designed to drive such a load will usually have an output impedance measured in hundreds of ohms.

If the load impedance is considerably higher than the source impedance driving it, it should be possible to split the source signal to drive two or more loads. However, you can't work the other way around and join two outputs together to mix them as the two output stages will try to dominate each other and the signal may be seriously distorted. In some cases, equipment may be damaged.

Don't worry if this seems a bit academic because modern-day recording equipment is invariably designed to interconnect without running into matching problems. If you have a cassette multitracker you should read the handbook to find out if you need to work with high- or low-impedance microphones. Apart from this, everything should work together quite comfortably. The basic rules on impedance matching are:

- When transferring a signal from one device to another the output impedance of the source device should be at least five times lower than the input impedance of the receiving device.

- A signal output may be split to feed two inputs, but a Y-lead should never be used to feed two outputs into one input. Two or more signals should only be mixed together using a mixer.

• When connecting loudspeakers to amplifiers the loudspeaker impedance should be as near as possible to the output impedance quoted for the amplifier.

There are two commonly-used standard operating levels: the -10dBV standard for semi-pro and domestic recording equipment and the +4dBu standard used with professional studio gear. These two levels are close enough to ensure that, as long as your gain controls are set correctly, they will usually still work together, although the meter readings between the two types of equipment will not agree. In theory mixing pro and semi-pro equipment will compromise your gain structure slightly, but in practice it proves that the deterioration in signal-to-noise ratio is insignificant.

decibels

Equipment specifications quote them, meters read them and operating levels conform to them, but what is a decibel, and where did they originate? Even though our VU meters are calibrated in decibels, even the most experienced engineer can start to fumble when asked to explain exactly what they are and how they are related to terms like dBu, dBm, dBv and dBV. It's all a throwback to the pioneering days of telephones, but at least it's a standard – of sorts.

The term decibel means a tenth of a Bel, named after Alexander Graham Bell, hence the capital B. Decibels don't necessarily relate to any fixed level of signal: the term is most often used as a convenient way of expressing the ratio between two signal levels. The decibel scale is logarithmic, just like the human ear, so decibels on a VU meter correspond pretty closely to our subjective impression of loudness.

The method of calculating decibels for ratios of both voltage and power is shown at the end of this chapter, and you might like to know that you can pick any power or voltage to be your 0dB reference level and then express all other values relative to that. For example, the recording-level meter on a tape machine is always set so that the optimum recording level is shown as 0dB, regardless of what that means in terms of magnetic flux at the record head. If a signal is lower than its optimum it is read as minus so many decibels, whereas if the signal is too high it is shown as a positive number.

Because decibels are logarithmic, most calculations involving them are concerned with addition or subtraction rather than multiplication or division. For example, a doubling of voltage corresponds to a 6dB increase and so quadrupling the voltage level would equate to a 12dB increase. As another example, a voltage amplifier with a gain of 60dB amplifies the input signal 1,000 times. The same is true of specifications such as dynamic range: a 100dB dynamic range means that the largest signal a circuit can handle is 100,000 times bigger than the smallest signal it can handle.

dBm

While decibels express only ratios, the dBm is a fixed value where 0dBm equates to one milliwatt of power dissipated into a 600ohm load. This is of little direct relevance in the world of modern audio, but it was vitally important in the pioneering days of telephone development when small amounts of electrical power had to be transmitted over long distances. 0dBm, then, refers to a signal of 0.775v applied to a load of 600ohms, which dissipates a power of 1mW.

Today the term dBm is often abused to signify a signal level of 0.775v, but unless the load impedance is exactly 600ohms this is technically incorrect. Because exact load impedances are less of an issue in modern audio systems, the new term dBu (with u meaning unloaded) was introduced to signify a voltage level of 0.775v, regardless of the load impedance. In other words, while the dBm is a measure of power the dBu is a measure of of only voltage. The term dBv (lower case v) also means the same thing as dBu, though the term dBu is more commonly used.

A standard reference voltage level of 0.775v is pretty clumsy when 1v would be easier to manage, which is where the recently-introduced dBV (with upper-case V) comes in: it signifies a signal level of 1V without regard to the load impedance.

standard levels

You may have heard it said that some recording equipment works at 'plus four' or 'minus ten', but what does this mean in practice? Plus four actually means +4dBu, an operating level adopted in pro audio due to historic rather than logical reasons and corresponding to an RMS signal level of 1.23v. This is a fairly convenient figure for use with modern op-amp circuitry as it leaves a sensible amount of headroom before the circuitry encounters clipping problems.

The minus ten level was introduced along with semiprofessional recording gear, and it is a largely Japanese concept. Correctly stated this is -10dBV, which corresponds to 0.316v, or just under a third of a volt. Again, this is reasonable for use with op-amp circuitry, but many purists feel that using the +4dBu system provides a better balance between noise and headroom.

A number of musical instruments, such as electronic keyboards, have an even lower -20dBV output level, which enables them to be used with domestic hi-fi equipment. Because of this, some effects units also have matching -20dBV low-level inputs, corresponding to a signal level of only 0.1v RMS. Using such equipment can cause problems, however, because a great deal of mixer gain is required to bring the signal up to a manageable level, with noise resulting as an unwanted side-effect. For this reason it may be a wise idea to use purpose-built keyboard pre-amps or DI boxes rather than to rely solely on the mixer line input to provide all of the gain.

calculating decibels

When comparing two power levels, the number of decibels difference may be calculated by the following equation:

Number of decibels = 10 log (P1/P2), where P1 and P2 are the two powers being compared and where the log is to the base ten.

Don't worry if you don't understand how logs work because few engineers actually get out their calculators when dealing with decibels. Instead, there are some useful figures that you should remember, the most common being that 3dB represents a doubling in power. It follows then that a 10W amplifier can produce 3dB more power than a 5W amplifier. Similarly, a 20W amplifier can produce 3dB more power than a 10W amp. So how much more powerful is a 20W amplifier than a 5W amplifier? The equation is simple: just add two lots of 3dB, which gives you 6dB.

Because of the mathematical relationship between power and voltage, the calculations are slightly different when it comes to working out voltage ratios in decibels. In this case the equation is:

Number of decibels = 20 log (P1/P2), where P1 and P2 are the two powers being compared, and where the log is to the base ten.

You'll notice that there is now have a 20 in the equation

instead of a ten, which means that the answer will be twice that of a ratio of powers. In other words, if the voltage is doubled the level goes up by 6dB, whereas if you halve the voltage the level consequently goes down by 6dB.

chapter 2

about mixers

Mixers are covered more thoroughly in the book *basic MIXERS* in this series, though you should find enough information in this chapter to get you started.

Whether you use an all-in-one cassette multitracker or a separate multitrack recorder and mixer, the mixer is the nerve centre of your studio: not only does it allow you to change the level and EQ of signals but it also provides a means of routing signals to and from tape or to external effects and processors. In principle, a mixing console is pretty straightforward, though I'd agree that large studio console can be intimidating at first. Even so, the principles are the same and the concepts embodied in a cassette multitracker's mixing section also apply to studio consoles.

Mixers comprise several identical building blocks known as channels, the purposes of a which is to change the level of the signal fed into them, to enable the signal to be EQ'd, and to provide routing. The process of routing includes sending the signal to what is known as a mix buss, an electrical circuit that allows the outputs from two or more channels to be combined to form a single, composite signal. To illustrate these concepts I'll describe a simple four-channel mixer, designed to mix four signals into one. Because the mixer has only one output, the output signal in this case will be in mono. For a stereo signal we'd need two signal paths: one to carry the left speaker signal and one to carry the right signal.

mic and line levels

In chapter one I emphasised that all electronic circuitry has an optimum operating range, and I introduced the idea of gain structure. Mixers are designed internally to work within a particular range of signal levels, usually up to ten volts or so. Some signals known as line-level signals fall within this range, such as the outputs from effects units, tape machines and many electronic instruments, but the signal produced by a microphone is at a level far lower than this. To bring the mic level up to the internal line level used by the mixer a low-noise microphone amplifier is inserted right at the input of the channel, and this may also be fitted with phantom power circuitry thus enabling it to be used with capacitor microphones.

phantom power

Capacitor microphones require power to operate, and phantom power is simply a standard method of sending 48v along the mic cable from the mixing console. Phantom powering can only be used with balanced microphones. As a rule, a microphone is balanced if the body is fitted with a three-pin XLR socket, but always check the data sheet that came with the mic to be sure. Use of unbalanced cables might cause damage to dynamic mics, as could plugging or unplugging them with the phantom power turned on.

channel gain

Because not all microphones produce the same level of output, and because the output level depends on the proximity and magnitude of the sound being recorded, the microphone amplifier is invariably equipped with a gain control that determines the amount of amplification applied to the signal. In other words, the setting of the gain control relates to how much the signal will be increased in level. Line-level signals don't need to pass through the microphone amplifier so mixer channels also have a line input. Normally only the line or mic input may be used, not both at once.

The line input on a typical mixer will also be fitted with a gain control, and on most professional mixers the mic and line inputs will have separate gain controls. On most home recording mixers and multitrackers, however, a common control is used for adjusting both mic and line gain.

mixer channels

Figure 2.1 shows a simplified schematic of a four-channel mono mixer with simple bass and treble equalisation. Separate mic and line gain controls have been shown clarify the setup, but in practice a single, shared control is more likely on a mixer of this type. There are separate input sockets for both the microphone and line-input signals, although on budget equipment it may be that a single socket will be used for both. A switch is sometimes used to select between the microphone input and the line input, but not always.

After input gain comes the EQ (equalisation) section, which can be as simple as the bass/treble (also known as hi/lo) arrangement shown here, or can be a complex multiband affair, as is more common in serious semi-pro and professional mixers. More sophisticated mixers have an additional switch which allows the equalisation section to be bypassed when it is not used.

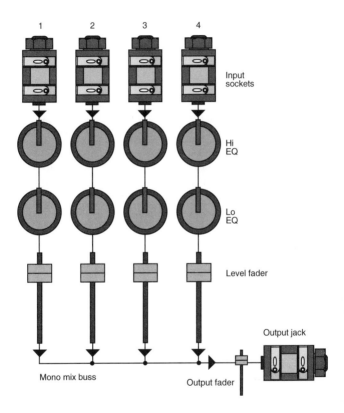

Figure 2.1: Simplified four-channel mono mixer

Finally, the signal level is controlled by a knob or fader before it passes to the mix buss, sometimes via an On or Mute switch. Note that all four input channels are identical, and a larger mixer would simply have more input channels.

The combined signal on the mix buss passes through another amplifier, known as the mix amplifier, which is controlled by the master level fader or knob. This controls the output level of the mixer, allowing it to present the correct signal level to the amplifier or tape recorder connected to the mixer. The master fader may also be used to make controlled fades at the ends of songs.

stereo mixers

A stereo mixer is only slightly more complicated than a mono mixer, as can be seen in Figure 2.2. This is very similar to the mixer shown in Figure 2.1 with the exception that the input channels have an extra control for panning the signal between the mixer's left and right outputs. When the pan (short for panorama) control is turned completely anticlockwise the channel signal is routed exclusively to the left mix buss, while turning it clockwise routes the signal to the right buss. Leaving the pan control in

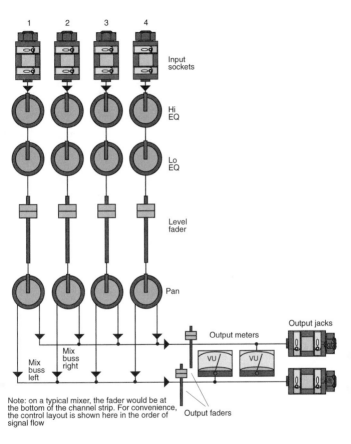

Figure 2.2: Stereo mixer with output meters

the centre routes equal amounts of signal to the left and right busses, making the resulting sound appear to originate from midway between the speakers when reproduced over a stereo speaker system. These two busses are often referred to in the singular as a stereo mix buss, though in reality the busses are physically separate devices.

In a stereo mixer there are two master faders, one for the left output and one for the right, though some mixers use a single stereo control to reduce the cost and size of the equipment. Figure 2.2 also shows a stereo-level meter, which allows the user to monitor the output level of the mixer. This will be familiar to anyone who has used a stereo cassette recorder, although the mechanism could take the form of a moving-coil meter with a physical pointer or a row of LEDs (Light-Emitting Diodes) arranged in the form of a ladder.

A simple mixer as so far described might be used in small PA applications, though the mixer section of a cassette multitracker isn't that different. A stereo mixer of this type is usually described in the form something into two – for example, a twelve into two (12:2) mixer has twelve input channels and two (left and right) outputs.

auxiliaries

In the studio we don't just want to mix and EQ signals; we also want to be able to add effects or send a mix to the performer's headphones. In a live situation a cue mix is required to feed to the stage monitors, and there has to be some way of providing a balance on the cue output that is different to that on the main stereo mix outputs. For example, singers usually need to hear more of the vocals than of the instrumental backing.

pre-fade send

Both effects and cue (sometimes called foldback) monitoring can be handled using the auxiliary controls on a mixer, and Figure 2.3 shows how these fit into the picture. Here you can see two new controls: Aux 1 and Aux 2, where aux is short for auxiliary. Aux 1 is simply another level control feeding a mono mix buss which runs across the mixer to the Aux 1 master level control and then to the Aux 1 output socket, but the signal feeding the Aux 1 control is taken before the channel fader and so is known as a pre-fade send. The implication of this is that the Aux 1 signal level doesn't change if the channel fader is adjusted. In other words, any mix set up using the pre-fade aux send will be completely independent of the channel faders. This is just what is required for setting up a cue mix for a

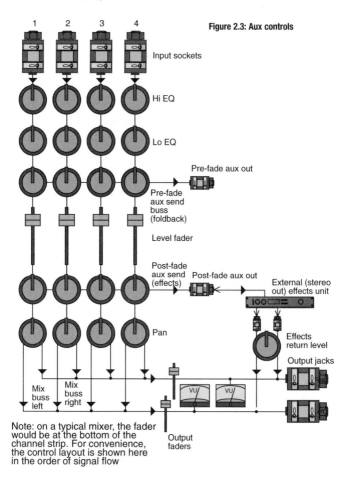

Figure 2.3: Aux controls

Note: on a typical mixer, the fader would be at the bottom of the channel strip. For convenience, the control layout is shown here in the order of signal flow

musician or singer performing an overdub. The overall Aux 1 mix controlled by the Aux 1 master level control, and the Aux 1 output would normally feed a headphone amplifier. Using a pre-fade send the engineer can provide the musician with a monitor mix that is exactly to his or her liking.

post-fade send

The second aux control, Aux 2, takes its feed from after the channel fader (post-fader), so its level is affected by any changes in the channel fader setting. This is exactly what we need if Aux 2 is being used to feed an external effect, such as reverb, because when the channel signal level is turned up or down we want the amount of effect to change by a corresponding amount.

By using different settings of the Aux 2 control on each channel it is possible to send different amounts of each channel's signal to the same effects unit. When the output from this effects unit is added to the main stereo mix this has the advantage that different amounts of the same effect can be added to different sounds in a mix. A typical example might be where one reverb unit is used to provide a rich reverb for the vocals, less reverb for the drums and little or none for the guitars and bass.

It is important to note that an effects unit used in conjunction with a channel aux send should be set up so that it produces only the effected sound and none of the original. This is usually accomplished by means of a mix control, which is either in the form of a knob or is accessed via the effects unit's editing software. In either case, the mix should be set to 100% effect, 0% dry (ie without effect).

effects returns

The output of the effects unit may be fed back into the mixer via spare input channels or dedicated effects return inputs, also known as aux returns. Aux returns are electrically similar to input channels but usually sport fewer facilities. They will have no mic inputs, and on a simple mixer they may have no EQ and no aux sends of their own. Normally they feed straight into the main stereo mix.

A spare input channel (or a pair panned hard left and right for stereo reproduction) may be used as an effects return, and here you gain the benefit of EQ and access to the aux send busses (for example, you may want to add reverb to the cue mix). However, you must ensure that the corresponding aux send (in this case Aux 2) is turned down on the return channel, or the effect signal will be fed back on itself, resulting in an unpleasant howl. The diagram in Figure 2.3 also shows how an external effects unit is connected. All of the controls shown in the figures are arranged in a logical order to illustrate the signal flow through the channel, though commercial mixers tend to have the pan and aux controls located above the channel fader for convenience.

insert points

Another way of connecting an effects unit or signal processor to a mixer is via an insert point. All serious stand-alone mixers have insert points on the input channels as well as on the master stereo outputs, though self-contained multitrackers don't always have them. An insert point is just a socket that allows the normal channel or stereo master signal path to be interrupted and re-routed through an external device. When no plug is inserted, spring contacts inside the socket complete the connection so that the signal flow is not broken.

On most home recording mixers the insert points are on stereo jack sockets, which means you need a specially wired Y-lead or adaptor to be able to use them. The stereo socket is conventionally wired 'tip send/ring return', with the cable screen being common to both send and return. Figure 2.4 shows the channel insert

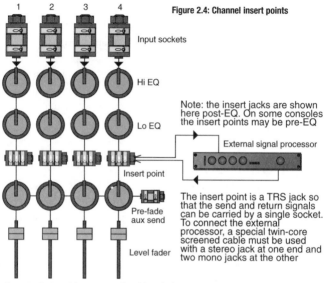

1 2 3 4

Figure 2.4: Channel insert points

Input sockets

Hi EQ

Lo EQ

Note: the insert jacks are shown here post-EQ. On some consoles the insert points may be pre-EQ.

External signal processor

Insert point

Pre-fade aux send

Level fader

The insert point is a TRS jack so that the send and return signals can be carried by a single socket. To connect the external processor, a special twin-core screened cable must be used with a stereo jack at one end and two mono jacks at the other

Pan control and busses omitted for clarity

points in a typical mixer. Physically they appear as stereo jacks and are usually found near to the mic and line input sockets.

effects and processors

This next paragraph is very important, and understanding its implications will save you a lot of trouble and frustration later on. While it is permissible to connect any type of effect or signal processor via an insert point, there are restrictions on what can be used via the aux send/return system. As a rule of thumb, only delay-based effects such as reverb, echo, chorus, phasing, flanging and pitch shifting should be connected via the aux system, and these are generally called effects. If the box uses delay to do its work then it's an effect, and if there's a dry/effect mix knob or parameter the box is also almost certain to be an effect. The unique quality of an effect is that it is added to the original signal. A process, such as EQ, isn't added to the original signal, but instead changes the original signal. Processors, such as compressors, gates and EQ, may only be connected via insert points, and under normal circumstances never via the aux sends and returns.

multitrack mixers

Cassette multitrackers have relatively simple mixer sections, and because everything is in one box there is no wiring to worry about other than plugging in the mics. Things become slightly more complicated with a separate mixer and multitrack recorder, but most of what you've already learned still applies.

As touched upon earlier, a studio console doesn't just mix signals – it also acts as a central routing system, sending signals to the different tracks on the tape machine, adding effects from external processors and mixing the outputs from the tape machine to produce a final stereo mix. At the same time, it has to function as a mixer within a mixer so that a separate control room monitor mix can be set up while the performers are recording or overdubbing.

tracks or channels?

The terminology associated with mixers can be a little confusing, and a common mistake made by even experienced users is referring to a mixer as having so many tracks. In fact mixers don't have tracks: they have channels (inputs) and groups (outputs). It's tape recorders that have tracks!

So far I've described a simple input channel with input gain, EQ, aux sends, pan control and a fader, but on a multitrack mixer there may be two different kinds of channel. The main input channel generally has the most comprehensive facilities and is used to feed microphones and line-level sources such as keyboards and samplers into the mixer while recording. When tape tracks are being mixed, the input channels handle the output from the multitrack tape machine.

The other type of channel is the monitor channel, so called because it is used to set up a guide monitor mix based on the multitrack recorder's outputs while the performers are overdubbing new parts. Without some way of hearing a mix of the tracks that have already been recorded there would be no way for the musicians to keep time, or stay in tune, with the music already recorded.

monitor channels

Monitor channels usually have fewer facilities than the main input channels because their main job is to provide a rough mix during the session. On a simpler mixer they may have little or no EQ and fewer aux sends than the main channel, though on an in-line mixer (so called because the main input and monitor controls are located in the same channel strip as the input channel controls) there's often provision to switch all or part of the EQ between the main and monitor signal paths, and the same is often true of the aux sends. To make this relationship easier to visualise, I like to think of the monitor section as being like a separate mixer connected to the tape machine outputs. The fact that the monitor section shares the same box as the main mixer (used for feeding stuff onto tape) is purely for convenience's sake.

Because the monitor mix is redundant when recording is complete, most mixers use the monitor channels as extra line inputs at the mixing stage. These may be used as additional effects returns or to add sequenced MIDI instruments, and they generally feed directly into the stereo mix.

groups

Up until now I've talked about mixers with simple stereo outputs, but for multitrack work it's necessary to have some way of routing different signals to different multitrack inputs at the same time. This is where the mixer group comes in. Whereas a stereo mixer just has a left and a right output, a multitrack mixer has several additional outputs, each with its own fader. These separate outputs are known as groups, and for use with an eight-track tape recorder, an eight-group mixer is ideal. The term eight-group mixer simply means that the mixer has eight mix outputs in addition to the main stereo output. Such a mixer may also sometimes be described as an eight-buss console because the eight groups are fed from eight mix busses.

Any of the input channels may be routed to any of the eight group outputs via routing switches which are linked to the eight group busses (as well as to the stereo output), and if two or more channels are routed to the same output they are automatically mixed together. As before the channel faders set the relative levels of the various elements in the mix, but now the group fader controls the overall level feeding the tape machine or other multitrack device. During recording the group outputs feed directly into the correspondingly numbered inputs of the multitrack tape machine, enabling any mixer input to be routed to any tape track without the need to replug any other cables.

routing

On a cassette multitracker, routing the desired input signals to tape is relatively straightforward as there are usually only four tracks to play with. On a multitrack mixing console, however, you'll find a set of routing buttons next to the channel faders, and these are used to send the channel signals either to the various group outputs (which are connected to the multitrack inputs) or to the stereo mix. At mixdown the stereo mix is used to feed the stereo mastering recorder, but the stereo output also feeds the control monitor during recording, overdubbing and mixing so that you can hear what you're working on.

pan and routing

Within each input channel a single routing button handles the routing for a pair of groups, with the pan control being used to change the balance of what is sent to the odd- and even-numbered groups. If you want to route a channel only to output Group 2, for example, you'd press the routing button marked 1/2 and turn the pan control fully clockwise so that all of the signal went to Group 2 and none to Group 1. Leaving the pan in its centre position would send equal amounts of signal to Groups 1 and 2. To record something in stereo (the different drum mics over a drum kit, for example) the relevant channels would be routed to a pair of groups and the pan control used to position the various sounds between them. The outputs from these two groups would then be recorded onto two tracks of tape. When being mixed, these two tape tracks would have to be panned hard left and right to maintain the stereo image created while recording.

routing buttons

On an 8-Group mixer, (the most popular format for project studio use) the routing buttons would be marked one to eight, with a further L/R button for routing the channel directly to the stereo mix. Figure

2.5 shows the flow of the signal through the routing buttons of a typical console, including the signal path to the group fader and the group output socket. Note that it's not necessary to use an eight-group mixer to work with an eight-track tape machine: you could use a four-group mixer as long as you don't need to record more than four groups at a time. You can still record more than four tape tracks at a time by using channel direct outputs, insert sends or even spare aux sends to feed additional tape tracks.

By connecting Group Output 1 to Tape Inputs 1 and 5 and Group Output 2 to Tape Inputs 2 and 6 and so on you can still record on all eight tracks without having to replug any cables. The tape machine record status buttons determine onto which of the two possible tracks each group will record.

split and in-line monitoring

On a conventional split mixing console the group faders and the monitor channel controls are situated on the right-hand side of the mixer. Between the main input channels and the monitor section is the master section, which includes functions such as the master stereo faders and the aux send and aux return master controls. On a more advanced mixer you'll also find

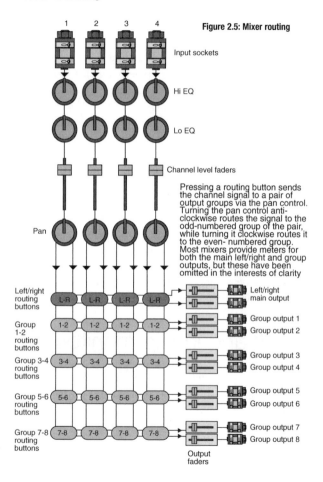

Figure 2.5: Mixer routing

Input sockets

Hi EQ

Lo EQ

Channel level faders

Pressing a routing button sends the channel signal to a pair of output groups via the pan control. Turning the pan control anti-clockwise routes the signal to the odd-numbered group of the pair, while turning it clockwise routes it to the even-numbered group. Most mixers provide meters for both the main left/right and group outputs, but these have been omitted in the interests of clarity

Pan

Left/right routing buttons

L-R · L-R · L-R · L-R — Left/right main output

Group 1-2 routing buttons

1-2 · 1-2 · 1-2 · 1-2 — Group output 1 / Group output 2

Group 3-4 routing buttons

3-4 · 3-4 · 3-4 · 3-4 — Group output 3 / Group output 4

Group 5-6 routing buttons

5-6 · 5-6 · 5-6 · 5-6 — Group output 5 / Group output 6

Group 7-8 routing buttons

7-8 · 7-8 · 7-8 · 7-8 — Group output 7 / Group output 8

Output faders

things like the test oscillator, the talkback mic, mix/two-track monitoring, headphone level control and other features. An eight-group console needs a minimum of eight monitor channels to provide an off-tape monitor mix, but many models have 16 monitor channels, allowing the mixer to be used with a 16-track recorder by using the split wiring arrangement described in Figure 2.6. The basic requirements for a monitor channel are level and pan controls, so that a stereo cue mix can be derived from the outputs of the multitrack recorder. In practice, however, most monitor channels have some form of basic EQ, along with aux controls

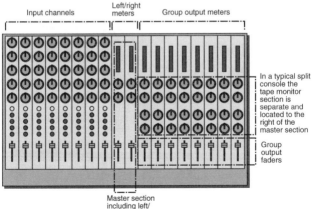

Input channels

Left/right meters

Group output meters

In a typical split console the tape monitor section is separate and located to the right of the master section

Group output faders

Master section including left/right master faders

Figure 2.6: Split-console arrangement

Sources to be recorded are
fed via the input channels

Figure 2.7: Signal flow during recording

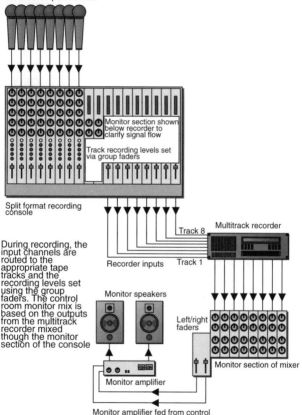

Monitor section shown
below recorder to
clarify signal flow

Track recording levels set
via group faders

Split format recording
console

Multitrack recorder

Track 8

During recording, the
input channels are
routed to the
appropriate tape
tracks and the
recording levels set
using the group
faders. The control
room monitor mix is
based on the outputs
from the multitrack
recorder mixed
though the monitor
section of the console

Recorder inputs   Track 1

Monitor speakers

Left/right
faders

Monitor section of mixer

Monitor amplifier

Monitor amplifier fed from control
room monitor output

that feed the same aux busses as the main mixer input channels. Figure 2.7 describes a multitrack mixer with the monitor section shown separately. In reality the monitor section is housed in the same box as the rest of the mixer, but it can help to visualised it as a separate mixer within a mixer. The diagram shows the signal flow during recording.

tape monitoring

Why is it that the monitor section always monitors the tape machine outputs? What happens if you want to hear what you're playing while you're recording it? Fortunately modern multitrack tape machines are far simpler than they used to be when there was a time delay between the record and playback head and when there were separate switches on the tape machine to switch each tape track between Input, Sync and Playback Monitor modes.

Modern tape machines take care of monitor switching without you even having to think about it, and the relevant signal is always present at the tape output socket. If a track is being recorded then you hear the tape input, but if the track is in Playback mode you hear what's on tape. However, older tape machines usually have a switch which allows each monitor channel to be fed from either the multitrack output or the group output (which is the same thing as the multitrack input).

console formats

Virtually all modern recording consoles adopt the in-line format, which differs from the split format in that the monitor controls reside in the same channel strip as the main input channel controls. On a split console the monitor section is usually in the master section or to the right of it, allowing it greater separation. In-line consoles may seem confusing at first, but the advantage of them is that, instead of being limited to just eight or 16 monitor channels, there's one monitor channel for every input channel. This layout usually results in a mixer that is deeper, front to back, than an equivalent split design, but it also it means the mixer can be made narrower for the same number of channels, which is an important consideration in a studio where space is limited.

mixing down

When mixing down on a split console all of the tape tracks have to be routed to the main Input channels the mix must be set up from scratch. On an in-line console, however, as each tracks is recorded a flip switch in the channel strip can be operated which routes the tape signal through the main input channel path, leaving the monitor input free for later use. The benefit of working this way is that you can be working on your mix and fine-tuning the balance and EQ as you go along. By the time you've finished recording you should have already set up the basis of a good mix.

monitors as line ins

Once the flip switch has been operated the monitor channels are connected to the console line inputs, allowing many line level sources to be fed into the mix. In these days of large MIDI systems, many of which are synchronised to tape, these additional inputs are a necessity rather than a luxury. Furthermore, these spare monitor channels may be used to handle extra effects returns if you run out of conventional effects return inputs. It's worth re-iterating at this point that an effects return is just another kind of input channel.

all-input mixing

Though both in-line and split consoles have separate

monitor channels to provide an off-tape control-room mix while recording, it seems that a great many people don't use them for that purpose at all. Instead they operate their mixers in all-input mode.

If you have an eight-track tape machine with enough mixer input channels you can leave the outputs of your tape machine permanently connected to the first eight channels of the mixer, routing these directly to the stereo left/right mix. The remaining channels may then be used to handle the signals which are being recorded. This removes the need to switch the off-tape signals between the monitor and input channels, and it also means that you can build up your mix, complete with added effects, as you record. In effect your control-room mix becomes your final mix.

The permanently-redundant monitor channels may then be used as inputs for MIDI instruments being sequenced in sync with the multitrack recorder or as effects returns. The only limitation of working in this way, other than having to ensure you have a mixer with enough input channels, is that the monitor channels can't be routed via the groups to create subgroups – they always feed directly into the stereo left/right mix. There's no right or wrong way to use your console – it's just a matter of finding a system that works for you.

subgrouping

Just as the monitor channels change roles when switching from recording to mixing, so does the group routing system. During recording, the groups are used to route signals to tape, but during mixing they can be routed back into the stereo mix. As always there's a very good reason.

Imagine that you have backing vocals recorded over four or five tracks of your multitrack tape. To change the overall level of the backing vocals you'd have to change the level by moving several faders at once, which is both cumbersome and inaccurate. A more effective approach is to create a subgroup of the backing vocals by routing the vocal channels to a pair of groups rather than directly to the left/right mix. In this way the whole stereo backing vocal mix can be controlled with just two group faders. Some consoles have the groups permanently routed to the stereo mix, while other provide Groups To Stereo buttons for each group fader, which generally route all odd-numbered group faders to the left and all even-numbered faders to the right.

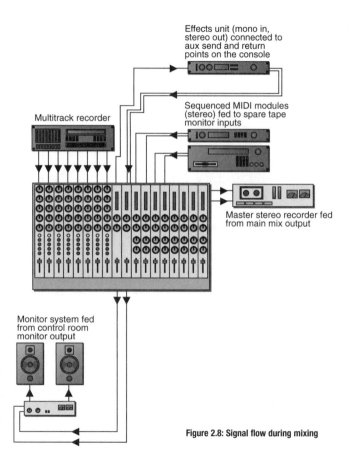

Effects unit (mono in, stereo out) connected to aux send and return points on the console

Sequenced MIDI modules (stereo) fed to spare tape monitor inputs

Multitrack recorder

Master stereo recorder fed from main mix output

Monitor system fed from control room monitor output

Figure 2.8: Signal flow during mixing

88

A better system – which is usually missing from budget consoles for cost reasons – is to provide group pan controls. If you have group pan controls you can create mono subgroups and still pan them anywhere in the stereo mix. If you don't have them you always have to use two group faders for every subgrouping operation, apart from those in which the end result will be panned either hard left or hard right.

In a typical mix you might create subgroups from drums, backing vocals and keyboards, which reduces the number of faders which need to be moved during the mix. Note that any effects that are to be added to these subgroups using the aux sends should be returned to the same subgroup (using the channel or effect return routing buttons) or the effect level won't change when the group fader is moved. Figure 2.8 shows the signal flow at mixdown. In this example, the monitor channels are being used as extra line inputs and the signal flow shows how subgroups actually work.

digital mixers

Digital mixers perform essentially the same function as their analogue counterparts. The main practical difference is in the user interface and the fact that many of their functions, including fader levels, can be automated. For more on digital mixers refer to the book on *basic MIXERS* in this series.

chapter 3

setting up a home studio

If you're new to recording a home studio can be a bewildering jumble of speakers, cables, boxes and winking LEDs. However, no matter how complicated the system, the essential components are roughly the same: you need to have a source of sound to record, such as the output from a microphone; you need a machine upon which to record; and you need some form of loudspeaker and amplification system to play back your work. At its simplest, you could make recording with just a stereo cassette deck, a pair of headphones and a couple of cheap microphones, but I'm assuming that people reading this book will be interested in multitrack work. These days it's very easy, and relatively inexpensive, to set up a combined MIDI and audio studio using a simple mixer, a computer and a suitable soundcard.

the components

The nerve centre in a commercial recording studio may be the mixing console, but if you have a cassette

Multitracker, Portastudio or one of the MiniDisc or hard-disk-based integrated multitrackers, the mixer and multitrack recorder are combined in a single piece of hardware. This not only makes the equipment smaller but also cuts down the amount of wiring required. It also sidesteps any potential matching problems that may arise between the recorder and mixer. The terms Multitracker and Portastudio are registered trademarks of Fostex and Tascam respectively, so I'll use the term multitracker with a lower-case 'm' to describe a generic combined multitrack recorder and mixer.

what else do you need?

You could just plug a microphone or two into your multitracker, put on a pair of headphones and start recording, but unless you want to work at a very basic level you're going to need some other hardware to go with it.

The first extra you're definitely going to need is a stereo tape machine or MiniDisc recorder on which to mix your finished recordings, and the better the machine the better the quality of your final recording. A good cassette deck will provide acceptable results for demo work, but if you want to try for more professional quality results then choose a DAT digital recorder or a

MiniDisc recorder. DAT machines are still the best option, and although they are rather more expensive than hi-fi cassette decks or MiniDisc recorders they can record at true CD (16-bit) quality.

Other possibilities when stereo mastering are to use the sound tracks of a hi-fi video recorder or to buy an open-reel stereo recorder, such as a used Revox or Tascam 32. Open-reel mastering machines have the advantage that you can edit your recordings on them using a razor blade and splicing tape. They also produce much better recordings than analogue cassette machines, and many professional engineers prefer the sound produced by them to that of digital tape.

Whatever mastering format to which you choose to mix down, the machine you use is known as a master recorder and the stereo mixes you produce are called master tapes. It is from these master tapes that any subsequent copies (or records and CDs) are made.

the monitoring system

Though headphones are useful in allowing you to continue working at antisocial hours, it's not a good idea to perform all of your recording and mixing on headphones as they often give quite a different impression to loudspeakers, especially when you're trying to evaluate bass sounds, and ideally you should check your work on both headphones and speakers. A stereo hi-fi amp of at least 30W per channel is recommended for home use, along with a pair of accurate loudspeakers. If you're going to use your hi-fi for monitoring as well as for playing records and CDS, ensure that your hi-fi amplifier has either aux, CD or tuner inputs that aren't in use – you can plug your multitracker's stereo monitor output into any of these. However, you can't use the phono record-deck inputs, as these have built-in tonal correction.

loudspeakers

No matter how sophisticated your studio, everything you do will eventually be judged by what comes out of your monitor loudspeakers. Choose the most honest-sounding speakers you can find, even if they don't offer the most impressive reproduction. Medium-sized two-way hi-fi speaker systems are usually fine for home recording, although dedicated near-field monitors tend to be more resistant to abuse. Whatever speakers you choose, try to listen to a selection of well-recorded CDs over them so that you become familiar with the way they sound. Your mixes are then more likely to be accurate, and they should also sound good on other hi-fi systems.

It also pays to double check your mixes on a cheap system, such as a ghetto blaster or a car stereo system.

microphones

You will to need at least one microphone to record vocals and acoustic instruments, and most studio setups will need more than one, especially if two or more performers need to record at the same time. Choosing the right microphone can be confusing, but as a rule it's best to use unidirectional (cardioid-pattern) mics unless you have a really nice-sounding room, in which case you could try an omni-pattern mic. As a rule, though, use dynamic cardioid mics (the same type as you'd use for live vocals) for recording electric guitars, bass guitars, drums and other loud instruments, but try to get hold of a capacitor mic to record vocals and acoustic instruments. Even the cheaper capacitor mics can be very good, but you will need a mixer that can supply phantom power in order to use them. If you don't have phantom power, consider using a battery powered back-electret mic instead.

You should also read the manual for your multitrack workstation before buying a mic to determine if you need to use high- or low-impedance mics. All professional mics are low impedance and balanced, though they can be used unbalanced with a suitable lead. If the mic has an XLR connector built into the handle and comes with a separate lead, it's almost certainly low impedance and balanced.

effects

Modern recordings make extensive use of electronic effects, even though this may not be obvious when listening to the record. The most useful effect is without doubt the reverb processor, but most of today's effects units provide a whole range of different effects for you to use. These are commonly known as multi-effects units because they can create more than one type of effect, and in general allow you to combine several effects at once. You'll need a minimum of one stereo reverb unit, but the ideal situation is to have at least one good reverb unit and one multi-effects unit.

the system

Figure 3.1 shows the connections of the various parts of a home-recording system based around an integrated multitracker. If you're using a hi-fi system to provide monitoring, the amplifier should be switched to Aux when recording and overdubbing, and to Tape when you want to hear your stereo mixes played back from

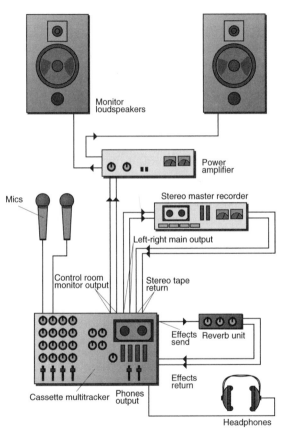

Figure 3.1: Recording system connections

the mastering machine. All cables should be kept as short as possible.

When setting up your studio, everything should be within reach and the speakers should be positioned symmetrically about the listening position. However, it's important not to place speakers too close to corners or the bass response will change unpredictably.

facilities

Studio effects can be very flexible, but you'll need a multitrack workstation or a separate mixer equipped with effects-send and -return facilities to make full use of them. Fortunately all but the very cheapest 'musical notepad'-type multitrackers have aux sends and returns. (If the term 'aux' is unfamiliar to you, refer back to the chapter on mixers.) Modern digital effects units have stereo outputs, so a multitrack workstation with at least one stereo aux return or two spare input channels is required for these.

The compressor is another signal processor without which it's hard to manage. A compressor is basically a device that automatically controls level and tries to smooth out the differences between the loud and quiet sounds, and most vocal tracks benefit from compression to keep them sounding even. If you intend to use a compressor you're best off having a multitracker with insert points on at least some of the channels. An insert point is a socket that lets you patch an external processor in line with the signal passing through the mixer channel.

You can't plug a mic directly into a typical compressor – or any other signal processor, for that matter – as they are normally designed for only line-level operation, but all is not lost if you have a system with no insert points. Instead of a regular compressor a voice channel-type device is required, on which a mic amp is combined with a compressor and sometimes an equaliser. These may be used to treat a mic signal directly so that the voice channel line output can be plugged into your mixer or recorder line input.

headphones

Although I've already pointed out that headphones are not great for critical mixing without at least double checking mixes on loudspeakers, they are absolutely essential for monitoring performers while overdubbing. In general, headphones may be either open (which allow outside sounds to filter in) or closed (which seal over the ears).

open headphones

Open or semi-enclosed hi-fi headphones usually sound most natural, but they tend to be bass light when compared to fully-enclosed headphones. High-quality headphones are particularly useful for checking stereo positioning and for picking up noises or distortion that you might miss when listening over loudspeakers. As long as you check your mix over loudspeakers at critical points, headphones can allow you to work at night and at other times when you might otherwise have to stop because of noise constraints. Open headphones are probably the easiest with which to work, though you'll need to double check the bass end of you mix using your studio monitors.

enclosed headphones

Enclosed headphones are preferred for monitoring while overdubbing because they don't allow much sound to leak in or out. Some of the better enclosed headphones are accurate enough for checking mixes, so if your budget only stretches to one pair a good enclosed pair might be the best option. However, you should try out as many as you can to hear how the sound compares with what you hear over loudspeakers. Check your multitrack workstation manual to determine the impedance of headphone that it can drive.

system connections

Most of the signal connections in a typical home studio are made using regular instrument jack leads or RCA phono hi-fi cables. Only microphones require special cables, although those that you'll need will depend on the input connectors of your mixer or multitracker. Very basic models may have inputs on jacks, whereas more advanced models will have balanced XLR inputs. All professional studio mixers have balanced XLR mic inputs. The multitrack workstation and cassette deck usually connect to the hi-fi power amplifier by means of standard RCA phono leads, though more professional amplifiers have balanced inputs on XLR connectors or balanced jacks leads.

Speakers should be connected using heavy, twin cable, not instrument coax leads. The speaker cables should be kept as short as possible and all the same length. There's no need to buy expensive speaker cable – what is most important is that it is thick enough to have a very low electrical resistance. Inadequate speaker cable will not only cause a loss of volume but the sound will also be compromised.

Setting up a system using a separate mixer and multitrack recorder isn't much more complicated, but you do need a bunch of cables to carry the mixer's group outputs to the multitrack machine's inputs and another bunch of cables to link the multitrack's output to the mixer's tape inputs. All signal cables between the mixer and the multitrack recorder must be screened.

mains wiring

In a typical studio there are lots of mains-powered boxes, but mains wiring should be kept as far away from the signal wiring as is practical, and if possible mains and signal leads should cross at right angles to reduce the amount of interference picked up from the 50Hz or 60Hz mains. The worst situation for interference is that in which mains and signal cables run alongside each other for any distance. In this case the signal cable tends to act as an antennae and picks up the hum radiated by the mains cable.

The earth leads should not be removed from any equipment that's supposed to be earthed, and mains plugs should be checked regularly – loose wires are not only dangerous but will also cause intermittent crackles and buzzes. The use of multiway mains distribution blocks is inevitable in the small studio (my own contains dozens of the things), but avoid plugging leads into and out of them too often as the socket spring will eventually go slack, which can result in bad contacts.

studio layout

As touched upon very briefly earlier on, you should set up your equipment so that it's easy to reach when in use. In a larger studio it may not be possible to reach everything, but you should at least be able to lay your hands on the controls you use most often. It's particularly important to sit in the correct position relative to your monitor loudspeakers when you're mixing. If you play keyboards or have a MIDI sequencer you'll also need to think about where to position these.

speaker placement

It's important to have the speakers set up symmetrically and in front of you, otherwise your stereo image will be affected; when using small speakers in a home studio, it's usually best to have them around one metre away and about the same distance apart, as shown in Figure 3.2. It's also advisable to keep the speakers at least half a metre away from corners, as speakers close to corners suffer an artificial increase in bass which may affect the way in which you mix. Speakers which are backed right up against a wall may also suffer an artificial increase in bass response. In a rectangular room it's usually best to position the speakers along the longest wall.

While it's quite common to see speakers standing on a shelf, on a table or on top of a mixing console, acoustically it's better if the speakers are on stands behind your equipment desk or mixer, as this cuts down on unwanted reflected sound. It's also better to mount the speakers upright rather than to lay them on their sides, as this will produce a wider listening area within which the mix sounds accurate. The optimum listening position is

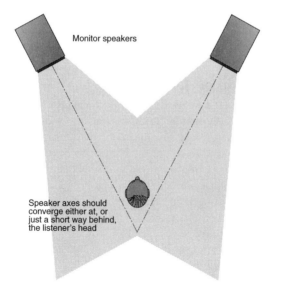

Monitor speakers

Speaker axes should converge either at, or just a short way behind, the listener's head

Figure 3.2: Monitor positioning

exactly between the speakers and is sometimes called the 'sweet spot'. To ensure that the sweet spot is as wide as possible, the speakers should be angled so that the tweeters point either at or just behind the listener's head, and the tweeters should be at head height or the speakers angled to point at the engineer's head.

acoustic treatment

Professional recording studios are designed to include elaborate acoustic treatment, but in the home studio there's usually insufficient money and space to add anything but very simple acoustic treatment. During the mixing process most problems are caused by loud reflections from the walls, floors and ceilings of a room, which confuse the direct sound of the speakers. From this you might rightly deduce that cutting down on excessive reflections is an obvious move, though you don't want to deaden your room so much that it sounds as though you're in a padded cell. Ordinary carpets, curtains and soft furnishings help enormously, and if you can hang heavy rugs or drapes on the rear wall, facing the speakers, this will deaden the sound even more.

It's important not to try to absorb too much reflected sound because bass frequencies are usually not as easily absorbed as high frequencies. If you add too much absorbent material the room is likely to sound dull and bassy, so it's best to aim for something like the acoustics of a domestic living room rather than something that sounds completely dead. A typical carpeted room should require little extra treatment. One of the benefits of near-field monitoring is that, because the speakers are physically close, you can hear more of the direct sound from the speakers and less of the reflected sound from the room, making room acoustics less of an issue. Also relevant is the fact the near-field monitors don't produce a lot of deep bass, and although heavy bass might sound impressive, unless the control room is acoustically treated the bass you hear is likely to be very misleading. It's much better to have an accurate sound with less bass.

If the room is excessively reverberant, try hanging a rug or a thick drape on the rear wall and two smaller ones on the side walls on either side of your normal listening position, as shown in Figure 3.3. If you can hang the rugs at around 30mm from the walls they will be more effective than if they were fixed directly to the walls. Foam acoustic tiles, or slabs of two-inch fireproof furniture foam, are also very effective at mid and high frequencies. Bedroom studios often work well with little or no extra treatment because the carpets, curtains and bed are very effective at absorbing sound. It should be noted that acoustic treatment is not the same thing as soundproofing. Hanging acoustic tiles around the walls or sticking egg boxes everywhere may change the acoustics of the room but it will do little to prevent unwanted sound from leaking in or out.

Figure 3.3 shows a possible studio layout incorporating a MIDI keyboard and sequencer with the position of additional absorbent material indicated. When a separate mixer and multitrack recorder are being used the layout is similar, with the mixer being at the centre of the action, though it may be more convenient to move the recorder to one side or the other.

patchbays

Patchbays often look daunting, but their sole purpose is to bring some degree of order to the potential wiring chaos of the recording studio. While many of the connections in a typical studio can be left alone, many more need to be changed on a daily basis. For example, you may have a compressor that needs to be patched into different mixer insert points as required, or you may want to move an effects unit from one send to another.

Rewiring a system without patchbays is awkward, mainly because most bits of studio gear have their connections at the back where you can't get at them

Figure 3.3: System layout example

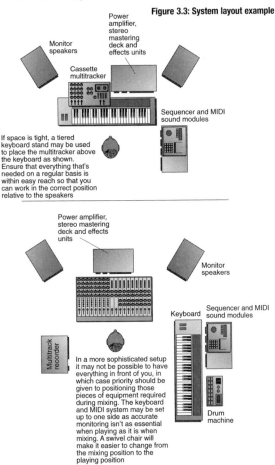

Monitor speakers

Power amplifier, stereo mastering deck and effects units

Cassette multitracker

Sequencer and MIDI sound modules

If space is tight, a tiered keyboard stand may be used to place the multitracker above the keyboard as shown. Ensure that everything that's needed on a regular basis is within easy reach so that you can work in the correct position relative to the speakers

Power amplifier, stereo mastering deck and effects units

Monitor speakers

Keyboard

Sequencer and MIDI sound modules

Multitrack recorder

Drum machine

In a more sophisticated setup it may not be possible to have everything in front of you, in which case priority should be given to positioning those pieces of equipment required during mixing. The keyboard and MIDI system may be set up to one side as accurate monitoring isn't as essential when playing as it is when mixing. A swivel chair will make it easier to change from the mixing position to the playing position easily. Similarly mixer insert points may or may not be accessible, depending on the make and model. Most use stereo jacks, however, so unless you have an endless supply of Y-leads or adaptors they're not easy to use, even if you can get to them.

A properly-organised patchbay will bring out all of your regularly-used audio connections to a single patch panel, enabling you to make any necessary connections by plugging in short patch cables. If you have any spare console sends and returns you could bring these out to the patchbay to enable you to patch in effects which clients or friends might bring round.

jackbays

At its simplest, a patchbay can be though of as a system of extension cables that bring the necessary input and output points to an easily accessible panel. Most semi-pro studios use standard jack patchbays because they are relatively inexpensive and because they interface easily with most musical and hi-fi equipment such as synths, effects pedals, guitar pre-amps, cassette decks and so on.

The most common form of jack patchbay uses standard jacks for both patching and rear-panel connections, which means that all of your system can be wired up with conventional jack leads, making it easy to reconfigure your patchbay when you want to integrate a new piece of equipment. So-called 'hard-wired' patchbays, in which the rear connections are soldered directly to the cable harness, are cheaper and arguably more reliable, but changing connections later is less straightforward. Currently the most popular type of jack patchbay fits a 1u panel and has two rows of 24 sockets. Convention dictates that the lower sockets are inputs and the top row are outputs.

Where a patchbay is used to provide access to the ins and outs of effects processors, the input channels of a mixer and so on, a basic non-normalised patchbay is required. In other words, the socket at the back of the patchbay connects directly to the socket on the front and nowhere else. Such a connection system is called non-normalised, and the sockets are purely extensions of whatever the patchbay is connected to.

normalising

In the case of insert points, another type of patchbay is necessary on which the upper and lower sockets are connected by means of normalising contacts when no patch plugs are inserted. The reason for this is related to the way in which console insert points are wired. Usually there's a stereo TRS insert jack socket on the console, which includes a pair of switch contacts so that the insert send is connected directly to the insert return if no jack is inserted. If this were not the case there would be no continuous signal path through the mixer channel, unless a processor was plugged into the insert point. The chapter on mixers explains insert points in greater detail.

Once a patchbay is connected to a mixer insert point, the mixer's internal signal path is broken because now there's a jack permanently plugged into the mixer insert socket. If nothing was done about this it would mean that whenever there was no processor plugged into the patchbay you'd have to use a patch cable to join the top and bottom sockets simply to complete the circuit. This would need a lot of patch leads and would make for a very congested patchbay, so normalised patchbays, with internal switch contacts, are used to do this automatically. When no connection is made to the patchbay the input jack is connected directly to the output jack.

semi-normal

In some circumstances it can be useful to take a signal from an insert send without breaking the signal path. For example, you might want to split a signal so that you can feed it both through the mixer channel and into a signal processor at the same time. The semi-normalised patchbay was developed to make this procedure easy: when nothing is plugged in, the patchbay output (insert send) is connected back to its input (insert return) via the normalising contacts. However, by fitting normalising contacts only the the lower (input socket), whenever a jack is plugged into the output socket only the input still remains connected to the output and the signal flow is not interrupted. Conversely, whenever a jack is plugged into the input (lower socket), the signal-path is broken. By using this type of patchbay you can plug into just the top socket to split the signal, or you can plug into both to connect a signal processor to the console's insert point.

The term 'sniff and break' is sometime used to describe this type of patchbay: plugging into the patchbay output socket allows you to 'sniff' the signal without affecting the existing signal flow, while plugging into the patchbay input breaks the signal flow. Semi-normalised sniff-and-break operation is now almost universal, even when the patchbay is said to be normalised, and there's no obvious advantage with a fully-normalised patchbay connection scheme. Most commercial patchbays include some form of link or other simple switching system to allow them to be configured for either semi-normalised or non-normalised operation. Figure 3.4 shows how both non-normalised and semi-normalised patchbay are wired, and if you only need a few patch points you could copy this wiring arrangement to build your own.

balancing

Once you get past the all-in-one multitracker level, most audio equipment is balanced. Balancing is a system that uses a screened cable with two cores rather than a single core (like a guitar lead, for example), the idea being that the any interference will affect both inner cores equally. Balancing electronics within the equipment at each end of the cable sends and receives the signals in such a way that interference on the two cores largely cancels out, while the wanted signal doubles in level. It's not essential to know exactly how balancing works, but you will need to use the correct cables when linking two pieces of balanced equipment.

Most home studios use unbalanced patching systems because most synths and pre-amps have unbalanced outputs. Insert points are also unbalanced on all but the very top-end pro studio consoles. However, if you want to use a patchbay to provide access points between the balanced outputs of a mixer and the balanced inputs of a multitrack recorder it's probably worth using a balanced patchbay. This will require stereo jack patch leads, though

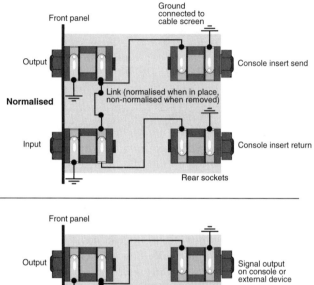

Front panel

Output

Normalised

Ground
connected to
cable screen

Console insert send

Link (normalised when in place,
non-normalised when removed)

Input

Console insert return

Rear sockets

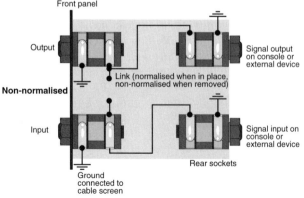

Front panel

Output

Non-normalised

Signal output
on console or
external device

Link (normalised when in place,
non-normalised when removed)

Input

Signal input on
console or
external device

Rear sockets

Ground
connected to
cable screen

Figure 3.4: Semi-normalised patchbay

most systems will allow you to use unbalanced mono jacks to feed unbalanced signals into a balanced input.

what to connect

It's always a good idea to bring out all of your console insert points to a semi-normalised patchbay, including the group inserts and the master (stereo output) inserts. If you don't want to wire up all of the channel inserts then you'll have to decide which channels you are likely to use for microphones and take their inserts to the patchbay so that you can patch in compressors when recording.

In more sophisticated systems it may be useful to connect a normalised patchbay between your mixer group outs and the multitrack inputs, allowing you, for example, to route a DI box or mic pre-amp directly to tape without having to pass the signal through the mixer. Similarly, you might want to use a semi-normalised patchbay to bring the multitrack returns back into the line inputs of the mixer, especially if your console has no Line/Tape switch.

As stated earlier, non-normalised patchbays are simple extension leads and are useful for bringing out the console line inputs, effects sends, effects returns and channel-direct outputs. Similarly, you could bring the inputs and outputs of all of your effects, processors and

MIDI instruments to a non-normalised patchbay. Other uses for non-normalised patchbays include line level 'tie lines', which are screened cables which run from your patchbay to a wallbox in the studio. These may be used for any type of general-purpose connection: for example, you might want to play a guitar in the control room but need to have it plugged into an amp in the studio. Similarly, you might have synths in the studio area that you want to plug into the mixer in the control room.

patchbay logistics

Plan the location of your patchbay to minimise the wiring connecting it to the rest of your equipment. As most patching involves the mixer and the effects rack it pays to keep them both as close to the patchbay as possible. Use good-quality screened cable to wire everything up and keep leads as short as possible. With insert Y-leads (with a stereo TRS jack at one end and two mono jacks at the other), consider buying the ready-made moulded varieties if you don't want to solder up your own.

For the patch leads, choose a soft, non-kinking cable or buy them ready made, and ensure that they're long enough to reach between the two furthermost sockets on your patchbay system. Coloured leads or plugs help in keeping track of your patching connections.

digital recording

Most modern recording equipment is digital, but to understand its strengths and weaknesses it's necessary to have some familiarity with analogue recording. Analogue tape recording has been with us for many years, but digital recording is a relatively recent development and is often misunderstood. In

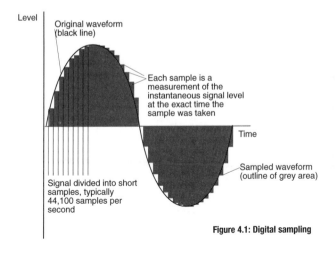

Figure 4.1: Digital sampling

some ways digitised sound is the audio equivalent to cine film, on which the constant motion of real life is represented by a series of still frames shown consecutively. As long as there are enough frames per second the human eye is deceived into perceiving continuous motion. When a sound is digitised it is also broken up into a series of frozen images, but, whereas cine can be made to work with just 24 frames of film per second, audio needs to be sampled at over 40,000 times per second, where each sample represents an instantaneous measurement of the voltage of the audio signal as shown in Figure 4.1.

sample rate

Physics dictates that audio must be sampled at a rate at least twice the maximum frequency to be stored, which for 20kHz audio means a sampling rate of at least 40kHz; however, for technical reasons concerning filtering, it's necessary to sample at a slightly higher rate. The CD format is based on a sampling rate of 44.1kHz, though some devices also sample at 48kHz. Esoteric devices can sample at 96Hz or even higher to increase the signal bandwidth. Sampling at a frequency lower than 40kHz means that the audio bandwidth is limited to less than the 20kHz required by professional audio equipment, but less demanding multimedia applications may sample at 32kHz or less so as to minimise the amount of data which needs to be stored.

bits

Sample rate determines the highest frequency we can digitise, but the accuracy of the individual samples depends on how precisely we can measure them. As a rule, the more bits are used to represent each sample the less noise and distortion there will be. CDs are sampled with 16-bit resolution, resulting in a possible signal-to-noise ratio of around 96dB (significantly better than analogue tape), but once again, for less demanding multimedia applications such as lo-fi computer games, eight-bit sampling may give acceptable results, though the signal-to-noise ratio will be reduced to a rather poor 48dB at best.

More professional audio formats use 20- or 24-bit sampling, but at the moment the CD format sets the standard at a 16-bit 44.1kHz sample rate. DAT machines are also 16 bit, with few exceptions, and usually offer playback at sample rates of both 44.1kHz and 48kHz, though the low-cost domestic models that find their way into home studios may record at only the 48kHz sample rate.

evolving digital

Whereas analogue tape recording was developed from the ground up as an audio recording medium, most of today's digital formats rely on technology from the computer, video and hi-fi industries. This makes manufacture commercially viable because of the economies of scale. Analogue recording has been refined over the past few decades to the point that it is unlikely that any further significant improvements will be made, and Dolby SR noise reduction may well be the last hardware breakthrough. By using the latest generation of high-energy tapes along with Dolby SR noise reduction, existing analogue recorders can provide a dynamic range approaching that of 16-bit digital recorders and, unlike other noise reduction systems, Dolby SR has virtually no audible side-effects. However, no analogue open-reel multitracks are now being built for the private studio market as the digital equivalent is much cheaper.

tape saturation

As mentioned before, analogue tape exhibits a magnetic saturation effect when overloaded, which has the result of causing a progressive increase in distortion at higher recording levels. This is rather more friendly than the hard clipping that occurs when digital systems overload, and indeed analogue tape saturation is often used deliberately to create warm sounding recordings. Analogue multitrack obviously still has a lot going for it, and even in this digital age many people still seek out well-maintained analogue machines specifically for their sound. Ironically, a number of digital processors and software packages are available which set out to process digital data in such a way as to emulate the effects of analogue tape saturation.

magnetic tape

All tape recorders suffer from the inherent disadvantage that the tape is in physical contact with the heads and guides of the machine, which wears down both the tape itself and the metal parts of the recorder. The other obvious disadvantage of a tape-based recording system is that winding the tape from one spool to another takes time.

Accepting the aforementioned limitations, and acknowledging that analogue recorders can sound exceptionally good, the actual results obtained depend on the electronic design of the recorder, the mechanics of the transport and the quality of the tape being used. If the tape is not moved across the heads at a perfectly constant speed then audible effects such as wow and flutter may be evident. The sound of a piano is a good test for wow and flutter because it has no natural vibrato. Analogue machines also suffer from modulation noise caused by the way the tape moves over the surface of the head, and although this isn't usually audible when recording music the chances are that, if you try recording a pure sine wave and then play it back, it will sound so jittery you'll think the machine is faulty. When you compare this with the same test done on a digital machine you'll wonder how analogue sounds as good as it does.

sound quality

The most significant factors affecting the sound quality of a well-maintained analogue recorder are tape speed and track width. The faster the tape passes over the heads and the wider the tracks then the better the sound quality. An analogue recording is made by magnetising millions of tiny particles of oxide as they pass over the record head, and so the recording can be considered as being the statistical summation of the magnetic charge of however many of these tiny magnets is passing over the head at any one time. The faster the tape, or the wider the tracks, the more particles per second pass over the heads and the more accurate the recording.

Narrow-format open-reel machines and cassette multitrack systems don't pass enough oxide over the heads over each second to produce an adequately low-noise floor, and so noise-reduction systems have to be employed. Unfortunately, all noise-reduction systems cause a deterioration in some aspect of the sound quality to a greater or lesser extent. Professionals tend to prefer working with two-inch tape running at 30ips (inches per second) without noise reduction, and on those occasions when noise reduction must be used, Dolby SR is the system of choice for professionals while, for the home user, Dolby S is generally regarded to be the best. Cassette multitrackers are often designed to run at twice the normal tape speed so that the selected noise-reduction system doesn't have to work so hard, but even a double-speed cassette runs at least four times slower, and has far narrower tracks, than a professional 15ips open-reel recorder.

Copying a recording from one tape track to another, as occurs during bouncing, causes a loss of quality. Every time an analogue recording is copied a little more noise is added and a little more clarity is lost. There can also be problems encountered when playing back tapes recorded on different machines because of small differences the alignment of the mechanical heads, causing a loss of high-frequency sound.

benefits of analogue

Having identified some of the weaknesses of the analogue system, it's only fair to look at the benefits. Analogue tape recorders have been around for a long time – they work, they're not too difficult to maintain and the tape itself is relatively cheap. Tape can be spliced, which makes editing easy, and recordings can be stored for many years with minimal deterioration, as long as they are stored in a suitable environment.

Because analogue tape can be overdriven without resulting in hard clipping you can be a little more casual about recording levels than you have to be with digital systems. Digital systems simply clip when overloaded, and unless the periods of clipping are extremely short the result is generally audible as a crackle or glitch. It's also possible to varispeed analogue tape over a very large range. If the worst comes to the worst and you have a problem with an analogue tape, such as dropout (usually caused by faulty tape or large pieces of foreign material on the heads), you can listen to the problem straight away and either redo the recording on a new tape or resort to performing cut-and-splice editing.

Deterioration caused by inappropriate storage is usually a gradual process and generally involves an overall loss of quality rather than a drastic and complete failure. For all of its operational crudities most audio professionals still seem to feel that analogue tape has the best sound on an artistic level, and they also have more confidence in its reliability than in digital tape and other digital, tapeless alternatives.

digital tape

There's a lot of rhetoric about the way digital recordings sound, but ultimately most serious music listening is done via compact disc, which is a 16-bit, 44.1kHz digital format with a theoretical maximum dynamic range of 96dB. Even though this is a better range than can be derived from analogue tape used with noise reduction, it's important to bear in mind that digital systems have no headroom at all above 0VU – there's no soft clipping as there is with analogue tape. For this reason, when working with digital multitrack, it may be necessary to set the nominal record level at around -12dB on the recorder's own meters, and even then you'll still need to keep an eye on the peaks. Once you've allowed a suitable safety margin (headroom), a 16-bit digital system may have little more usable dynamic range than a good analogue recorder working with Dolby SR. Even 20- and 24-bit machines are limited by the analogue circuitry in their converters, so why is everyone going digital? Perhaps digital systems produce less distortion?

more on sampling

We know that digital recording systems work by sampling the instantaneous level of the input signal thousands of times a second and then storing these samples as binary numbers. The number of bits defines the precision with which each sample can be taken, and because every sample can only be measured to the nearest whole bit the digital representation of an analogue waveform is really a series of tiny steps, as shown in Figure 4.1. In the case of a 16-bit system, a full-scale signal would occupy two to the power of 16 (or 65,536) steps, and if the signal being recorded is large it will use most of the available bits and so be adequately accurate. However, smaller signals will be represented by fewer bits, and so the lower the signal level the higher the percentage of distortion. Analogue tape machines work the other way round: the distortion increases as the level increases. Note that these steps aren't present in the output signal, as filters in the digital-to-analogue converter smoothe them over.

Another benefit of digital systems is that no noise-reduction system is required to achieve a greater than a 90dB signal-to-noise ratio, and, because digital machines are driven from a very accurate crystal-controlled clock, there's no mechanism by which the recording rate can drift, unlike analogue, where an imperfect capstan shaft or worn pinch roller can compromise the performance. Even with a budget digital system, wow and flutter is effectively eliminated because the digital data goes to and from tape via a crystal-clocked memory buffer.

by the numbers

Once a recording is in the digital domain it's really just a catalogue of numbers. This is rather like storing a piece of line art as a precision 'join-the-dots' drawing. Because we're dealing with absolute numbers it's possible to copy the data from one digital machine to another, or from one track to another, simply by duplicating these numbers. The result is a perfect copy with no loss in quality – provided that none of the numbers are inadvertently changed.

error correction

In the real world a few of the numbers occasionally get lost or altered when a transfer takes place, but digital recorders use a very powerful error-correction system to enable them to reconstruct small amounts of damaged data, and so loss of accuracy is only a problem when something is seriously wrong with either the hardware or the tape. This error correction is vitally important to offset the destructive effects of particles of dirt on the tape's surface and to compensate for minor tape dropouts.

The ability to make a near-perfect clone of digital data is of immense value when mastering to DAT, or when multitracking on something like the Alesis ADAT or Tascam DA-88, because a second machine will allow you to make safety copies just in case anything should happen to the original.

what can go wrong?

Both analogue and digital tape formats are fine when they're working properly, but what happens when a tape becomes worn or a machine goes out of alignment? With an analogue machine alignment errors usually lead to a fall off in the high-frequency response of the recording, while a damaged tape may result in momentary dropouts (brief but audible drops in level and/or high-end frequency response). Digital machines, on the other hand, deal with absolute numbers, and because some errors are inevitable due to dust on the tape, head wear and imperfections on the surface of the tape, their error-correction systems are constantly checking for and repairing corrupted data. A system of recording redundant data enables the machine to verify the data integrity by means of checksums, and small errors can be repaired completely by using the redundant data to reconstruct the original data. This is made possible because the recording process distributes the data on the tape in such a way that a brief dropout causes a multitude of small errors over a short period of time rather than causing a large cluster of adjacent errors. If the data were to be recorded in a linear fashion, a single dropout would be irretrievable because all of the errors would be in one place.

error concealment

Errors involving a greater amount of data corruption may not leave sufficient information for the error correction to reconstruct the original. It's rather like jabbing a number of small holes in the page of a newspaper: if there are only a few holes you can work out the missing letters from the context of the undamaged text surrounding the holes, but as the number of holes increases you'll eventually get to a point where you don't have enough undamaged text to be sure about what's missing. You may still be able to guess, but at some point even guessing will become impossible.

When this happens to audio data, the system moves from error correction mode to error concealment. In effect the software examines the data each side of the problem section and uses interpolation to construct a plausible replacement for the missing data. This technically causes a brief rise in distortion, although it's usually too brief to be audible. If longer errors occur then the system can't even make a rough guess as to what's missing, so it mutes the audio output until more readable data comes along. Only at this point do you notice that something is wrong.

While error correction is a wonderful ally it also prevents us from seeing problems develop until it is too late, unless the equipment concerned has some form of error readout system. Sadly most home studio equipment has little or no error readout facility, and the first you know that anything is wrong is when you hear a dropout. Because head wear or recorder mis-alignment can cause data corruption or misreading problems it is very important to have digital tape machines serviced on a regular basis, even if no problems are apparent. Most DAT and digital multitrack tape machines should be serviced every 500 hours.

Digital tape can't be edited by using razor blades in the same way as analogue tape. Editing can be achieved by cloning data from one digital machine to another, but this is time consuming and not everyone has access to two machines. In fact the only really satisfactory way to edit digital material is to use a hard-disk editing system, and these are described later in this chapter.

For routine work where little or no editing is needed, analogue tape is probably still the easiest medium to use and it has fewer complications. Digital tape recording is a seductive concept, but inexperienced users might find that their recordings are just as noisy as they were originally because the major source of noise isn't usually the recording system, it's the material being fed into it. However, digital tape has the advantages that recordings can be cloned, there's no wow and flutter, and the media cost is low.

DCC

Before leaving digital tape recording systems, it is appropriate to mention the Philips DCC (Digital Compact Cassette) format. This is a consumer system that uses data-reduction algorithms to simplify the audio signal to the extent that it can be recorded onto tape by means of a stationary multi-channel head. The result is technically inferior to DAT and CD inasmuch as data reduction can be shown to have audible side-effects with some types of material, but to put it in perspective the side-effects are less serious than those encountered with most types of semi-pro (and indeed most professional) analogue tape noise-reduction systems. The vast majority of people are unable to differentiate between DCC and CD on commercial pop music, but classical music recordings may show up a lack of detail or a reduction in the sense of space.

At the time of writing the remaining DCC machines are being sold very cheaply, as they have not been a commercial success. They are a viable pieces of equipment, however, and a far superior option to analogue cassette recorders in a home studio environment. If you can obtain a machine, make sure that you buy a good stock of blank tapes as no one is sure how long the format will be supported. The digital data from a DCC machine can be transferred to DAT machine, but DCC can't be used for backing up digital data from hard-disk recorders because of the data-reduction algorithms used.

MiniDisc

Like DCC, Sony's MiniDisc system used data compression to fit an entire CD's worth of material onto a disk less than half the size. MiniDisc seems to have caught on in the consumer marketplace, and so seems assured of a reasonably long life. Small portable models are available, which are suitable for mobile sound gathering, and multitrack machines based on the technology offer up to eight tracks of high-quality audio.

hard disk recording

Even as recently as the early 1990s tapeless recording was too expensive for most home recording enthusiasts to contemplate, but now the cost of the hardware has plummeted to the point where it's probably the cheapest way to get into multitrack recording – and it looks set to continue getting cheaper. Using a computer such as a G3 Macintosh, or a Pentium II or III PC fitted with a suitable soundcard and a large-capacity hard drive, you can experiment with tapeless recording and editing for little more than the cost of the computer and some software.

Alternatively there are stand-alone hard-disk-based digital workstations and recorders which don't rely on a computer for their operation – they're more like the tapeless equivalent of an integrated multitracker or multitrack tape machine. The reason why prices have fallen so significantly is that, unlike analogue recording, the hardware used in tapeless systems is based on the same components used elsewhere in the computer industry, and the demands of multimedia keep pushing the price down and the quality of performance up.

tapeless quality

Even basic 16-bit hard-disk recording can provide the same audio quality as CD, and indeed the quality may be better than digital tape because hard disk error-correction systems are always more rigorous. However, audio fidelity is also dictated by the quality of the analogue-to-digital and digital-to-analogue converters used in the product. For example, high-quality converters in an external rack box are likely to sound every bit as good as a CD, while budget converters residing in a computer, either as part of the basic hardware or on a soundcard, are much more likely to pick up noise from the computer's own electronics. They may also use cheaper converter chips which offer relatively poor resolution, resulting in increased noise and distortion. As with other aspects of digital systems, converters are improving at an impressive rate.

hard drives

Tapeless multitrack recorders usually store their data onto computer hard drives or onto some form of removable disk. Currently, not all hard disk drives are suitable for recording multitrack audio, though most new computers come equipped with so-called AV drives, which can usually handle up to at least 16 tracks of simultaneous playback. Older computer drives take short breaks to recalibrate themselves to offset the effects of temperature changes, and while the buffer memory may be large enough to ensure that this doesn't interrupt the data flow you may hear breaks in the audio if you're recording or playing back more than a couple of tracks. The problem increases proportionally with the more tracks you intend to play back at once time, which is why AV drives were developed. These have intelligent thermal recalibration systems that avoid interrupting when the disk is reading or writing data, making them a better choice for multitrack work. Most modern drives are AV compatible, but some models are faster than others. As a rule, the higher the speed of the disk spindle the faster the access time.

random access

Computer hard drives can move to any piece of data within a few milliseconds, which is a great benefit for audio users. Random access means that you don't have to wait for tape to wind forward or backward to get where you want to go, but the advantages of random access go much further than simply avoiding tape rewinding time. By using RAM memory as a buffer, audio can be read onto and from a disk in a continuous, uninterrupted stream, which opens up all kinds of interesting editing possibilities. For example, you can access any section of recorded audio data in any order, rearrange the sections into a new order and then play back your new arrangement.

destructive editing

Being able to rearrange, copy or remove material without altering the original data file is known as non-destructive editing, and there's a lot you can do to a recording without changing the original data in any way. Nevertheless, there are times when you may want a change to become permanent – for example, when silencing the noise immediately prior to the start of a song or changing the actual level of the recorded audio. On a computer-based system you may even be able to zoom in on a tiny section of the audio waveform to wipe out an annoying guitar squeak or similar noise.

The main editing tricks of which digital systems are capable are based around rearranging material in a different order, but you can also normalise signal levels to bring the peaks up to 0dB, apply digital EQ, reverse sections of sound, create fade-ins and -outs, along with number of other functions that would have been difficult or impossible using tape. More sophisticated systems allow you to use plug-in software-based effects (the software equivalents of separate signal processors or effects units), such as reverb, delay, compression, stereo enhancement, de-noising, click removal, 3D spatial enhancement and so forth.

media costs

Disks are currently only a little more expensive than tape (a two-inch reel for use on a 24-track machine costs around £100 and holds little more than 40 minutes of audio). One minute of mono audio requires around five megabytes of drive space, though this can be reduced by up to a factor of four if a data-compressed audio format is used. It isn't practical to archive to fixed disk drives in the same way as it is to tape, but it's possible to use a tape-based data backup system, such as Exobyte or data DAT. Alternatively CD-Rs or write-once DVDs are cheap (albeit non-rewritable) backup options.

audio with MIDI

The ability to record audio directly onto the hard drive of an ordinary computer gets really exciting when you combine it with MIDI. Virtually all leading sequencer manufacturers now produce software packages that integrate the recording and editing of MIDI data with the recording and editing of audio. In other words, any audio you record can be accessed and arranged in much the same way that you would arrange your sequenced MIDI patterns, from the same sequencer arrange page. Everything is done from the same computer, and you don't have to keep changing your mental outlook as you switch from working with MIDI data to audio data.

If you already work with MIDI then adding a few tracks of direct-to-disk audio is a very practical and flexible way of installing a complete recording studio on your desktop. Little additional hardware is needed (the audio is automatically synchronised to the MIDI data), and even 'virtual' effects can be added inside the computer provided that you have the right software and a sufficiently powerful computer. Even a reasonably sophisticated system is only likely to need the addition of a small mixer, a few synth modules and one or two effects boxes. Furthermore, because a typical MIDI composition may only include a small amount of audio, removable media drives become more cost-effective as a storage medium.

hard disk editors

Hard disk editors exist specifically to manipulate and rearrange stereo material, and they are most commonly used in compiling individual tracks to produce a production master tape for an album project or in rearranging the sections of a song to create a new version. Such editing systems are often used to create extended remixes or to shorten songs. Sophisticated cross-fading algorithms are used to ensure that there are no audible glitches at the edit points, which is something that isn't always true when editing analogue tape using razor blades. Tapeless editing may also be used to assemble the best parts of several different versions of the same piece of music or dialogue.

While basic cut-and-paste editing is possible on a multitrack hard disk system, a dedicated stereo-editing system or software package will usually include specialist tools that can be used to edit audio to a much finer degree, though the features of both multitrack systems and editors are now staring to converge. Other software tools include utilities for PQ coding CD masters (adding the pause and cue information) and for burning writable CDs to produce one-off CD masters from your DAT original.

practicalities

With any computer-based audio recording system it's advisable to use a separate drive to store your audio. Audio drives need to be emptied or defragmented pretty regularly, and if you keep all of your other software and system files on the same drive this becomes more difficult. With a separate drive all you need to do is back up finished projects and then erase all of the data on the drive ready for the next session.

Stereo material sampled at 44.1kHz uses around ten megabytes of disk space per minute (add 50% to this for 20- or 24-bit recordings), which means that approximately 600Mb of disk space is required to record an hour's worth of stereo material. In reality rather more is required because, if you decide to perform a destructive edit, the system usually creates backup files so that any changes that don't work out as planned can be undone. For this reason, a one-gigabyte drive should be considered the absolute minimum for editing a typical album project, though with drive prices as low as they are a four-gigabyte drive or larger is a better bet. As a rule larger-capacity drives are also faster, which means that you can record and play back more tracks simultaneously in a multitrack system.

With multitracking, available disk space is shared out between however many tracks you want to record, so it follows that the recording time available is halved every time you double the number of tracks. Using a three-gigabyte drive you can expect to get over an hour of continuous eight-track or more than 30 minutes of 16-track recording time, even leaving 10% of the drive unused, as the speed of the drive should be kept high.

input/output options

The way in which audio gets in and out of your system depends on the your hardware. Low-end soundcards often have only analogue inputs and outputs, while more sophisticated cards may include S/PDIF and/or AES/EBU digital interfaces. As long as the analogue inputs are of reasonable quality they'll probably be fine for multitrack work – after all, most of the source material is analogue. However, when editing stereo material it's generally considered unacceptable to leave the digital domain, unless you specifically need to treat the audio material using an analogue processor of some kind.

The audio data to be edited is generally fed in from DAT via the digital I/O connectors, but it's advisable to buy a proper digital transfer cable. While you may get away with using a hi-fi phono lead, you could equally end up with inexplicable clicks and glitches! Cards with ADAT and T/DIF interfaces are available for connecting to digital multitrack machines or digital mixers that support the same interface formats.

integrated tapeless workstations

Hard disk recording systems require DSP power to process audio data, and the more processing you need to do at one time the more processing power is required. Some card-based systems allow you to add more DSP power in the form of additional cards, either fitted inside the computer or in an expansion chassis. Nevertheless, such systems are currently expensive and are more likely to appeal to professionals able to make a commercial return on their investment.

The other option is to choose a hardware-based audio workstation which combines tapeless recording, mixing and effects. These tend to have fewer features than their computer-based cousins but they are invariably more straightforward to use, and the usual minefield of computer problems and conflicts is neatly avoided. More importantly, if it stops working you know where the blame lies, whereas if a computer system packs in the software manufacturer will probably blame the hardware and vice versa!

Currently, cassette-based multitrackers are being superseded by Data MiniDisc-based eight-track machines. Data MiniDiscs are more cost effective to archive than any other form of removable media presently available. MiniDisc uses an aggressive data-compression system to maximise the recording time available from a disk, but in reality the side-effects of data compression are far less serious than those of the analogue tape noise-reduction systems that went before. While uncompressed audio remains the preferred choice for professional applications, formats like MiniDisc provide an affordable alternative for the private studio owner or recording musician.

future systems

In the future we'll probably see more computer-based, direct-to-disk systems connected to dedicated hardware-control surfaces so that they combine the advantages of the digital environment with the control surface of a conventional analogue-style mixer. Such interfaces are available now, but they tend to be expensive. However, as computers become more powerful, the need for hardware control will become greater and market pressure should result in cheaper user interfaces.

Once again, the multimedia market will probably be largely responsible for the next generation of products, and already it's possible to perform even more sophisticated multitrack recording and editing using nothing more than an off-the-shelf multimedia PC and a suitable software package. However, media compatibility is likely to remain a major issue as new drive formats appear on a monthly basis, few of which are compatible with their predecessors. There will also be serious clock synchronisation issues to be addressed once fully digital recording systems, comprising multiple separate pieces of equipment, become commonplace in the private studio. In a professional studio, all pieces of equipment are synchronised to a single master clock, but semi-pro equipment doesn't always have a wordclock sync facility.

In the longer term we can expect solid-state rather than disk storage, but in the shorter term I believe that analogue tape, digital tape and disk-based recording will continue to co-exist amicably for a number of years yet.

chapter 5

recording and mixing

Recording and mixing is covered in more depth in other books within this series, but the following chapter contains some basic information that will ensure that you get off to a good start. It doesn't matter whether you're using analogue tape, digital tape or a tapeless system – the same basic rules apply.

Once your system is up and running you'll probably want to carry out an experimental recording session to see how it all works. It helps to get organised: label your tapes, make up track sheets for each song and include notes on any MIDI instruments that are being used.

Analogue recorders should be cleaned before you start the session (see the end of this chapter), while digital tapes should be formatted. Ensure that your instruments are working properly, with no hums or buzzes, and check the states of guitar strings and drum heads and so on so that there'll be nothing to distract you once you start recording. Also, keep an electronic tuner handy and check guitars between each take. Most guitars drift out of tune as the room warms up. Modern keyboards are OK, but analogue synths should be switched on well before the session starts and checked regularly.

When you're setting up your mixer, take care that only the channels you need are routed to tape – it's easy to end up recording things that you didn't intend to because a routing button was accidentally left down or a fader left up. It's particularly easy to make this kind of mistake when track bouncing, so always double check your routing and then listen to what you've recorded to make sure it's what you wanted.

If you have a multitrack mixer with routing it helps to separate groups of sounds into subgroups so that the mix can be handled with fewer faders. For example, if the recording has real drums, these are likely to occupy several tracks so it makes sense to assign them to a single, stereo subgroup. Other candidates for subgrouping are backing vocals and multilayered keyboard parts.

miking

Vocals should be miked from around nine inches, with a pop shield between the mouth and the mic. A pop shield can simply be a pair of tights stretched over a wire hoop positioned halfway between the mouth and the microphone. Without this, the mic will almost certainly pop on 'P' and 'B' sounds. If the room is too live, hang up some blankets to the sides of and behind the singer.

Guitar amps are best miked with a dynamic mic very close to the grille, while basses may be DI'd or miked from around six inches away. Keyboards are invariably DI'd, and with the new generation of recording pre-amps guitars may be DI'd too.

Drum kits are best miked with dynamics mics close to each of the drum heads, usually a couple of inches away. The kick drum is miked using a dedicated bass drum mic inside the shell, aimed at the pot where the beater hits the head. A cushion or blanket can be used to damp the drum, and the front head must have a hole in it).

The overall sound of the kit is best captured by positioning a pair of capacitor mics a few feet above the kit and separated by around five feet. This gives a good stereo image that helps bind the close miked sound together. It also captures the cymbals and hi-hats.

If you don't have enough mics to record each drum separately, use just a kick drum mic and the stereo overheads. This will give you more of a live sound, but it can be very effective, especially in a flattering-sounding room.

track allocation

If you're starting out with a system that can only record eight tracks or so you'll need to plan your recording carefully in advance. Live band recordings need to be done with most, if not all, of the members playing together, but you may have to submix some of the sounds so that they share a track, especially if you're multimiking a drum kit. Try to lay down a guide vocal as you play, even though this will be replaced later, as it'll help everyone to know where they are during overdubbing. Its best to add instrumental solos later, and because they usually come between vocal sections you can often get away with recording the solo on the same track as the vocals, if tracks are limited.

If bouncing is necessary, try to bounce things that aren't main components in a mix. For example, you can usually get away with bouncing backing vocals or pad keyboard parts, but bouncing drums or main vocals is to be avoided where possible.

Getting the best possible vocal recording is important,

so do what you can to make the singer feel comfortable. This includes giving them a good headphone mix, usually with some reverb added.

mixing

Any mixer or multitracker will enable you set up a stereo mix from your recorded tracks, complete with pan, EQ and effects-send settings, but you still need a stereo recorder to record that mix. Though you can create demos using a hi-fi cassette deck, DAT machines are better as they record CD-quality sound onto an inexpensive digital cassette. They operate much like conventional cassette recorders, though you should watch the meters to prevent clipping on signal peaks. MiniDisc is also a viable mastering option for home use, though it isn't as accurate as DAT because it uses data compression.

When all the overdubs are complete and you're ready to mix, set all the aux sends to zero and set all EQ controls (or their on-screen virtual equivalents) to their central or neutral positions. MIDI or SMPTE sync signals should not be fed via the mixer because of the danger of crosstalk when high-level sync codes are used. It is always best to use separate external cables to route the time code track from the tape machine to the synchroniser.

Set up your balance in mono to start with, and only start thinking about panning the sounds once a good balance has been achieved. Effects should be added last of all.

If MIDI instruments driven directly from a sequencer feature in the mix, these may be fed into any spare mixer input channels or even into spare aux returns. If you don't have enough spare channels then you may have to think about using an external keyboard submixer.

balance

On mixers with PFL buttons, the PFL metering system should be used for each input channel in turn to optimise the gain setting; the PFL meter should just go into the red on signal peaks.

Try not to monitor too loudly as this will affect your judgement and may eventually damage your hearing. The most logical monitoring level would be at the same level at which the end user is likely to listen – in other words, a sensible domestic listening volume.

Set up the drums and bass balance first, as these form the rhythm section for your track, then add the vocals and other instruments. Once the mix is working in mono, work on the stereo panning. Bass drums, bass guitars, bass synths and lead vocals should be left in the centre, while the other instruments and effects can be spread out to give your stereo recording some width. Reverb should always be added in stereo, as this makes a huge contribution to the way the mix is perceived. Most digital reverberation units have a mono input and a stereo output, and those with stereo inputs tend to use a mono mix of the left and right inputs to create the reverb, with only the original sound being passed through in stereo. This means that, no matter where in the mix the original signal is panned, its reverb will come equally from both sides. Don't worry that you're not making full use of your stereo-mixing capabilities simply because so many of your sounds are located at or near the centre of the mix. You only need to move a couple of sounds out to the sides to create a sense of space, and the addition of stereo reverb will greatly contribute to the sense of width.

Most engineers add compression to the vocals in order to keep their level even throughout the mix. A ratio of around 3:1 is usually effective, with the threshold adjusted until around 6dB of gain reduction is taking place. Use auto attack and release if you have it, or set a fast attack and around half a second of release.

effects with delay

Try panning a signal to one side of the mix with a delayed version (5-50ms) panned to the other side. The sound will appear to be coming from the speaker that's carrying the unprocessed sound even if the delay is as loud as the original signal, and although the psycho-acoustic reasons why this is so are rather too complex to go into here it does provide another way of adding space to a sound. If the delay is then modulated to produce a chorus sound the resulting effect is the illusion of movement, and when listening in stereo you really can't tell that one channel is carrying a dry sound and the other a processed version, as the movement seems to occupy the whole of the space between the speakers.

Delay can of course be used to create more conventional effects involving echo and doubling, and it has become fashionable to set up delay times that are multiples of the tempo of the song. For example, if a song is running at 120 beats per minute, each beat is 60 divided by two seconds long, which is half a second. Therefore a delay of 500m (half a second), 250ms or 125ms will always create echoes that are in time with the music. You can also divide the beat time into threes to create echoes that occur in triplet time.

the door test

One trick used by many professionals is listening to the mix from outside the studio with the door open. In this way, anything that is too loud or too quiet will stand out very clearly. It's also a good idea to play some commercial recordings through your studio monitoring system before mixing so that you have a general sound to aim for.

Level adjustments are often necessary during the mix, but don't change the level of the drums or bass as this will make your rhythm section sound unstable. If you're not using a computer with mix automation and you have a lot of adjustments to make, get somebody to help you with the final mix and use a wax pencil to mark the faders settings for different points in the song.

stereo checklist

- Pan bass instruments and bass drums to the centre of the mix. Snare drums tend also to work best when panned near the centre, but the toms and cymbals may be spread (not too widely) from left to right.

- Keep the lead vocals close to the centre of the mix as they are the focus of the performance, but experiment with positioning backing vocals to the sides.

- When you pan an instrument away from the centre of the mix don't always feel that you have to set it hard left or right. Try to paint a picture with your sounds, spreading them across the stereo stage in interesting ways and the main sounds nearest the centre.

- Take care not to pan stereo mics or the outputs from a stereo instrument (such as a piano or drum kit) so wide as to produce the illusion of an instrument that is as wide as the stage!

- Unless you're specifically trying to create a special effect you should pan the outputs from your stereo reverb unit hard left and right to ensure that they are at the same level in the mix.

- Use your discretion when panning the outputs from stereo effects units such as delays and chorus units. Consider panning them over just half of the stereo soundstage – between dead centre and hard left, for example.

problem mixes

Probably the most common technical problem is noise, which could includes tape hiss, instrument amplifier hiss, amplifier hum and general digital noise from budget synths and effects units. You can attack noise problems on several different levels, and if the contamination is serious you may need to use two or more of the following processes in combination.

A noise gate is a very effective way of removing noise during the pauses between sounds, and you'd be surprised at how much you can clean up a mix by gating any channels containing parts that aren't playing all the way through the mix. For example, if the lead guitar solo only pops up in the middle of the song you don't want any background noise on that track contributing to the mix the rest of the time, so bang a gate on it. It's also often worth gating vocals because there are usually pauses between words or phrases in which nothing useful is happening. However, don't feel that you have to gate out traces of breath noise, or the vocal track may well end up sounding unnatural.

With any slowly decaying sounds, make sure that you set an appropriately long gate release time. Even if some gated sounds appear to be slightly unnatural, there's a good chance that they'll sound OK when reverb is added, especially when the rest of the mix is being played.

corrective EQ

Changing the EQ of a signal is obviously going to have some effect on the overall sound of that signal, but quite often you'll find that your mix includes sounds that occupy only a limited part of the audio spectrum. For example, the overdriven electric guitar contains no really deep bass and the top end rolls off very quickly above 4kHz or so because of the limited response of a guitar speaker. This being the case, you can apply a sharp top cut above 4kHz and a low cut below 100Hz without changing the sound significantly. You'll have to experiment to find the exactly frequencies, but you'll find this technique very useful, not only with guitars (and bass guitars) but also with warm synth pads from cheap or vintage instruments. Careful use of EQ may also help to reduce the effect of finger noise on guitars and other stringed instruments.

treating the mix

The sound of a completed mix can be made richer with the use of compression, which is usually connected via the mixer's master stereo insert points. As a rule, a soft-knee compression with a low ratio (less than 1.5:1) and a low threshold (around -30dB) works best.

EQ

Equalising the whole mix can improve the sound: boost at 80Hz to beef up bass drums and basses, cut at around 200-250Hz to reduce boxiness and apply broad-band high EQ at around 15kHz to add sparkle. Be careful not to apply too much EQ, however, and if you feel that something sounds fine as it is then there's nothing wrong with leaving it alone.

Once you've made your master tape, check it on as many different sound systems as you can to ensure that the balance is OK. Listening in the car is always a good test.

cleaning tape machines

Analogue tape and cassette machines should be cleaned before every recording session. It only takes a few moments and it really helps in optimising the sound quality, as well as making your tapes and heads last longer. Digital machines are less easy to clean thoroughly, so have the job done professionally every few months. Head cleaning tapes may be used occasionally.

Clean the heads and tape with isopropyl alcohol and cotton buds, then dry then with a clean cotton bud. If more brown oxide comes off, clean them again. Rubber rollers should be cleaned using water with a little washing up liquid added to it – alcohol can damage the rubber if used too often.

common cable connections

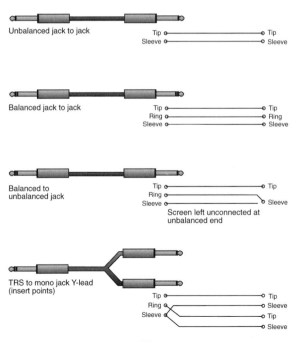

Unbalanced jack to jack

Tip o——————o Tip
Sleeve o——————o Sleeve

Balanced jack to jack

Tip o——————o Tip
Ring o——————o Ring
Sleeve o——————o Sleeve

Balanced to
unbalanced jack

Tip o——————o Tip
Ring o
Sleeve o——————o Sleeve

Screen left unconnected at
unbalanced end

TRS to mono jack Y-lead
(insert points)

Tip o——————o Tip
Ring o——————o Sleeve
Sleeve o——————o Tip
——————o Sleeve

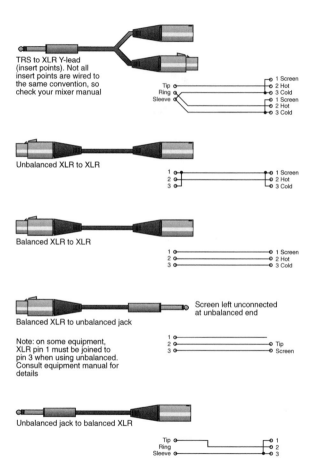

TRS to XLR Y-lead
(insert points). Not all
insert points are wired to
the same convention, so
check your mixer manual

Tip
Ring
Sleeve

1 Screen
2 Hot
3 Cold
1 Screen
2 Hot
3 Cold

Unbalanced XLR to XLR

1
2
3

1 Screen
2 Hot
3 Cold

Balanced XLR to XLR

1
2
3

1 Screen
2 Hot
3 Cold

Balanced XLR to unbalanced jack

Screen left unconnected
at unbalanced end

Note: on some equipment,
XLR pin 1 must be joined to
pin 3 when using unbalanced.
Consult equipment manual for
details

1
2
3

Tip
Screen

Unbalanced jack to balanced XLR

Tip
Ring
Sleeve

1
2
3

glossary

audio
Area of technology related to sound recording, processing, amplification and reproduction.

active
Circuit containing transistors, ICs, tubes and other devices that require power to operate and are capable of amplification.

ADSR
Envelope generator with Attack, Decay, Sustain and Release parameters. This is a simple type of envelope generator and was first used on early analogue synthesisers, though similar envelopes may be found in some effects units to control filter sweeps and suchlike.

ADT
Automatic Double Tracking, a term used to describe the use of a short echo to simulate the effect of the same sound being recorded twice. See Double Tracking.

AES/EBU
Digital interfacing standard for transferring stereo audio data from one system to another. Connection standard is a balanced XLR, and regular mic cables may be used for short-distance

communication, but specialised digital cable is recommended.

AFL
After-Fade Listen, a system used within mixing consoles to allow specific signals to be monitored at the level set by their fader or level control knob. Aux sends are generally monitored AFL rather than PFL so that the actual signal being fed to an effects unit can be monitored.

algorithm
Computer program designed to perform a specific task. In the context of effects units, algorithms usually describe a software building block designed to create a specific effect or combination of effects. All digital effects are based on algorithms.

ambience
Result of sound reflections in a confined space being added to the original sound. Ambience may also be created electronically by some digital reverb units. The main difference between ambience and reverberation is that ambience doesn't have the characteristic long delay time of reverberation – the reflections mainly give the sound a sense of space.

amp
Unit of electrical current, short for ampere.

amplify
To increase the amplitude (magnitude) of an electrical signal.

amplitude
Another word for level. Can refer to levels of sound or electrical signal.

analogue

Circuitry that uses a continually-changing voltage or current to represent a signal. The origin of the term is that the electrical signal can be thought of as being analogous to the original signal.

attack

Time taken for a sound to achieve maximum amplitude. Drums have a fast attack, whereas bowed strings have a slow attack. In compressors and gates, the attack time equates to how quickly the processor can change its gain.

attenuate

To make lower in level.

audio frequency

Signals in the human audio range, nominally 20Hz to 20kHz.

aux

Control on a mixing console designed to route a proportion of the channel signal to the effects or cue mix outputs (see Aux Send).

aux returns

An aux return is, in effect, an additional line input channel but with fewer facilities than the main input channels. On smaller mixers they will be permanently routed to the stereo mix buss, while larger desks will provide the same routing arrangement as on the main input channels. Though these are included for use with effects, they can be used to add any line level signal (such as from a tape machine, CD player or MIDI instrument) to the mix.

aux sends

Mixers invariably incorporate both pre-fade and post-fade aux sends. Aux sends provide a means to set up an independent mix of the channel signals, either for feeding effects or for providing a foldback mix. Pre-fade sends aren't affected by changes in the position of the channel fader, which makes them ideal for setting up foldback mixes. Post-fade sends are derived after the channel fader, so if the channel fader is adjusted the aux send level changes accordingly. This is necessary when adding effects such as echo or reverb because the relative levels of the dry signal and the effect are usually required to remain constant.

balance

This word has several meanings in recording. It may refer to the relative levels of the left and right channels of a stereo recording, or it may be used to describe the relative levels of the various instruments and voices within a mix. When balanced equipment is connected onto both ends of the cable, any interference affecting the cable is cancelled out, resulting in a cleaner signal. Most microphones used in recording are balanced.

band

A specific range of frequencies. In audio, this usually means a section of the audio spectrum.

bandwidth

Means of specifying the range of frequencies passed by an electronic circuit such as an amplifier, mixer or filter. The frequency range is usually measured at the points where the level drops by 3dB relative to the maximum.

binary

Counting system based on only two numbers: 1 and 0.

bit
Binary digit, which may either be 1 or 0.

boost/cut control
single control which allows the range of frequencies passing through a filter to be either amplified or attenuated. The centre position is usually the 'flat' or 'no effect' position.

bouncing
Process of mixing two or more recorded tracks together and re-recording these onto another track.

BPM
Beats Per Minute.

buffer
Section of computer RAM memory used for temporary storage of information. The term may also be used to describe an analogue circuit designed to isolate the effects of one circuit from another connected to it. For example, a buffer circuit on the output of one device may be used to prevent the next piece of equipment in line from loading the output of the first device.

buffer memory
Temporary RAM memory used in some computer operations, sometimes to prevent a break in the data stream when the computer is interrupted to perform another task.

buss
An electrical signal path onto which other signals may be mixed. In a mixer or multitracker different busses are provided to carry the stereo mix, the signals being mixed to tape, the

aux sends and so on. The term is also used for power cables that supply numerous destinations (for example, to the individual circuit boards inside a mixer).

byte
Piece of digital data comprising eight bits.

C-60
Cassette tape designed to provide a total of 60 minutes playing time when used in a conventional cassette deck. When used in a multitracker, the maximum playing time will be reduced to 30 minutes because the tape is played only in one direction (it is not turned over when it reaches the end). In some multitrackers, the tape speed is double that of a hi-fi machine in order to provide higher sound quality. This halves the maximum playing time again meaning that a C-60 tape will provide a maximum of 15 minutes' recording.

cable
Insulated electrical conductor (for example, a power cord or signal lead).

cannon connector
Proprietary brand of XLR connector.

capacitor
Electronic component comprising two spaced conductors coupled electrostatically. The space between the conductors may be air or some other non-conducting dielectric.

capacitor microphone
Professional recording microphone that works by small

changes in electrical capacitance. Capacitor microphones require phantom power to operate, usually 48v.

cardioid microphone
Meaning heart shaped, describes the polar response of a unidirectional microphone.

channel
In the context of MIDI, a channel refers to one of 16 possible data channels over which MIDI data may be sent. The organisation of data by channels means that up to 16 different MIDI instruments or parts may be addressed using a single cable.

channel
In the context of mixing consoles, a channel is a single strip of controls relating to one input.

chase
Term describing the process whereby a slave device attempts to synchronise itself with a master device. In the context of a MIDI sequence, Chase may also involve chasing events – looking back to earlier positions in the song to see if there are any program changes or other events that need to be acted upon.

chorus
Effect created by doubling a signal and adding delay and pitch modulation.

click track
Metronome pulse which helps musicians to keep time.

clipping

Severe form of distortion which occurs when a signal attempts to exceed the maximum level which a piece of equipment can handle.

clock

Electronic circuit designed to generate precisely-spaced pulses for timing applications, such as analogue-to-digital conversion or driving a digital processor.

compander

Encode/decode device that compresses a signal while encoding it, then expands it when decoding it.

compressor

Device designed to reduce the dynamic range of audio signals by reducing the level of high signals or by increasing the level of low signals.

conductor

Material that provides a low resistance path for electrical current.

console

Alternative term for mixer.

continuous controller

Control providing smoothly variable control rather than obviously switched steps. Of course, in digital circuits and in MIDI all changes are made up of discrete steps, but as long as the changes between successive steps are small enough the result is perceived as being continuous.

control voltage

Control Voltage. Used to control the pitch of an oscillator or filter frequency in an analogue synthesiser. Most analogue synthesisers follow a one volt per octave convention, though there are exceptions. To use a pre-MIDI analogue synthesiser under MIDI control, a MIDI-to-CV converter is required.

CrO_2

Type of recording tape based on a chromium oxide compound, also known as Type II. Most multitrackers are designed to give the best results with Type II tapes.

cut-and-paste editing

Copying or moving sections of a recording to different locations.

cycle

One complete vibration of a sound source or its electrical equivalent. One cycle per second is expressed as one Hertz (Hz).

daisy chain

Term used to describe serial electrical connection between devices or modules.

DAT

Digital Audio Tape. The most commonly-used DAT machines are more correctly known as R-DATs because they use a rotating head similar to that in a video recorder. Digital recorders using fixed or stationary heads (such as DCC) are known as S-DAT machines.

data

Information stored and used by a computer.

data compression

System for reducing the amount of data stored by a digital system. Most audio data compression systems are known as lossy systems, as some of the original signal is discarded in accordance with psychoacoustic principles designed to ensure that only those components which cannot be heard are lost.

dB

Decibel. Unit used to express the relative levels of two electrical voltages, powers or sounds.

dBm

Variation on dB referenced to 0dB = 1mW into 600 ohms.

dBv

Variation on dB referenced to 0dB = 0.775v.

dBV

Variation on dB referenced to 0dB = 1V.

dB/octave

A means of measuring the slope of a filter. The more decibels per octave the sharper the filter slope.

dbx

A commercial encode/decode tape noise reduction system that compresses the signal during recording and expands it by an identical amount on playback.

DC

Direct Current.

DCC
Stationary-head digital recorder format developed by Philips. Uses a data-compression system to reduce the amount of data that needs to be stored.

DCO
Digitally-Controlled Oscillator.

decay
Progressive reduction in amplitude of a sound or electrical signal over time. In the context of an ADSR envelope shaper, the decay phase starts when the attack phase has reached its maximum level. In the decay phase, the signal level drops until it reaches the sustain level set by the user, and then remains there until the key is released, at which point the release phase is entered.

depth
The amount by which one parameter is modulated by another (for example, vibrato or chorus depth).

desk
Alternative word for mixer or console.

DI
Direct Inject, in which a signal is plugged directly into an audio chain without the aid of a microphone.

DI box
Device for matching the signal-level impedance of a source to a tape machine or mixer input.

dielectric

Insulating layer between the two conductors of a capacitor.

digital audio
Electronic device that works by representing electrical signals as a series of binary numbers.

digital delay
Digital processor for generating delay and echo effects.

digital reverb
Digital processor for simulating reverberation.

DIN connector
Type of multipin connector with several possible pin configurations. MIDI uses a five-pin 180° DIN plug and socket.

disc
Format of data storage, such as CD or MiniDisc. Excludes computer floppy and hard disks, which end with the letter k to signify that that they are abbreviations of the word diskette.

disk
Abbreviation of diskette, but now used to describe computer floppy, hard and removable disks (see Floppy Disk).

disk drive
Mechanism for reading and writing computer floppy or hard disks. Fixed hard drives include a disk that cannot be removed.

display
Computer monitor or some form of alphanumeric readout built from LCDs or LEDs.

distortion

Any measurable difference, other than in amplitude, between an input signal and an output signal.

dither

System of adding low-level noise to a digitised audio signal in such a way that extends the low-level resolution at the expense of a slight deterioration in noise performance.

Dolby

Type of tape noise-reduction system. Dolby B, C and S are used in both hi-fi and semi-pro recording equipment, while Dolby SR and Dolby A are only used in professional applications.

double tracking

Process of recording the same performance twice, onto two different tape tracks. When the two parts are played back the effect of two people playing or singing together is created. Double tracking is often used to thicken up the sound of a weak vocalist.

driver

Term used to describe the mechanical part of a loudspeaker. Also used to describe a piece of software that enables a hardware peripheral or internal card to interface with a computer.

drum pad

Synthetic playing surface which produces electronic trigger signals in response to being hit with drumsticks.

dry

Signal to which no effects have been added. Conversely, a sound which has been treated with an effect, such as reverberation, is referred to as wet.

dubbing
Adding further material to an existing recording. Also known as overdubbing.

dynamic microphone
Type of microphone that works on the electric generator principle, whereby a diaphragm moves a coil of wire within a magnetic field.

dynamic range
Range in decibels between the highest signal that can be handled by a piece of equipment and the level at which small signals disappear into the noise floor.

dynamics
Method of describing the relative levels within a piece of music.

echo
Effect created by repeating the original signal, often several times, after a short time delay.

edit
To change recorded data or computer-stored digital data in some way.

effect
Device designed to add special effects to a sound. Examples

include delay, reverb, pitch shifting, chorus, flanging, ADT, phasing and vibrato.

effects loop
Connection system that allows an external signal processor to be connected into the audio chain.

effects send
Mixer output designed to feed a signal to an external effects unit.

effects return
Additional mixer input designed to accommodate the output from an effects unit.

electret microphone
Type of microphone based on a permanently-charged capacitor capsule.

encode/decode
System that requires a signal to be processed prior to recording, which is then reversed during playback.

enhancer
Device designed to brighten audio material using techniques such as dynamic equalisation, phase shifting and harmonic generation.

envelope
The way in which the level of a sound or signal varies over time.

envelope generator

Circuit capable of generating a control signal which represents the envelope of the sound you want to recreate. This may then be used to control the level of an oscillator or other sound source, though envelopes may also be used to control filter or modulation settings. The most common example is the ADSR generator.

equaliser

Device for selectively cutting or boosting selected parts of the audio spectrum.

event

In MIDI terms, an event is a single unit of MIDI data, such as a note being turned on or off, a piece of controller information, a program change, and so on.

exciter

Enhancer that works by synthesising new high-frequency harmonics.

expander

Device designed to decrease the level of low-level signals and increase the level of high-level signals, thus increasing the dynamic range of the signal.

expander module

Synthesiser with no keyboard, often rack mountable or in some other compact format.

fader

Sliding potentiometer control used in mixers and other processors.

ferric

Type of recording tape composition. Ferric tapes are usually the cheapest but don't produce as high a quality result as CrO_2 or Type II tapes.

file

Meaningful list of data stored in digitally. A Standard MIDI File is a specific type of file designed to allow sequence information to be exchanged between different types of sequencer.

filter

Electronic circuit designed to emphasise or attenuate a specific range of frequencies.

flanging

Modulated delay effect using feedback to create a dramatic, sweeping sound.

floppy disk

Computer disk that uses a flexible magnetic medium encased in a protective plastic sleeve. The maximum capacity of a standard high-density disk is 1.44Mb. Earlier double-density disks hold only around half the amount of data.

foldback

System for feeding one or more separate mixes to the performers for use while recording and overdubbing. Also known as a cue mix.

format

Procedure required to prepare a computer disk for use. Formatting organises the disk's surface into a series of electronic pigeonholes into which data can be stored. Computers with different operating systems often use different formatting systems.

frequency

Indication of how many cycles of a repetitive waveform occur in one second. A waveform which has a repetition cycle of once per second has a frequency of 1Hz.

frequency response

Measurement of the frequency range that can be handled by a specific piece of electrical equipment or loudspeaker.

FSK

Frequency Shift Keying. A method of recording a sync clock signal onto tape by representing it as two alternating tones.

fundamental

Any sound comprises a fundamental or basic frequency plus harmonics and partials at a higher frequency.

gain

Amount by which a circuit amplifies a signal.

gate

Electronic device designed to mute low-level signals, thus improving the noise performance during pauses in the wanted material.

general MIDI

Addition to the basic MIDI specification designed to assure a minimum level of compatibility when playing back GM-format song files on different machines. The specification covers type and program, number of sounds, minimum levels of polyphony and multitimbrality, response to controller information and so on.

glitch
Describes an unwanted short-term corruption of a signal, or the unexplained short-term malfunction of a piece of equipment. For example, an inexplicable click on a DAT tape would be termed a glitch.

GM reset
Universal Sysex command which activates the General MIDI mode on a General MIDI instrument. The same command also sets all controllers to their default values and switches off any notes still playing by means of an All Notes Off message.

graphic equaliser
Equaliser on which several narrow segments of the audio spectrum are controlled by individual cut/boost faders. The name derives from the fact that the fader positions provide a graphic representation of the EQ curve.

ground
Electrical earth, or zero volts. In mains wiring, the ground cable is physically connected to the ground via a long conductive metal spike.

group
Collection of signals within a mixer that are mixed and then routed through a separate fader to provide overall control. In

a multitrack mixer, several groups are provided to feed the various recorder track inputs.

hard disk
High-capacity computer storage device based on a rotating rigid disk with a magnetic coating onto which data may be recorded.

harmonic
High-frequency component of a waveform at a multiple of the fundamental frequency.

harmonic distortion
Addition of harmonics not present in the original signal.

head
Part of a tape machine or disk drive that reads and/or writes data to and from the storage media.

headroom
The safety margin in decibels between the highest peak signal being passed by a piece of equipment and the absolute maximum level the equipment can handle.

HF
High frequency.

high-pass filter (HPF)
Filter which attenuates frequencies below its cutoff frequency.

hiss
Noise caused by random electrical fluctuations.

hum

Signal contamination caused by the addition of low frequencies, usually related to the mains power frequency.

Hz

Shorthand for Hertz, the unit of frequency.

impedance

Can be visualised as the AC resistance of a circuit which contains both resistive and reactive components.

inductor

Electrical component, usually some form of coil, that exhibits inductance. Inductors have a higher impedance at high frequencies than they have at low frequencies.

initialise

To automatically restore a piece of equipment to its factory default settings.

insert point

An insert point is simply a socket at which the signal flow may be interrupted, allowing an external signal processor to be connected – for example a compressor or gate. Most consoles use TSR stereo jacks as insert points, which means that a Y-lead is needed to connect the external device. Alternatively, the insert points may be wired to a normalised patchbay. Insert points are usually provided in the input channels, the groups and at the main L/R stereo outputs.

insulator

Material that does not conduct electricity.

interface
Device that acts as an intermediary to two or more other pieces of equipment. For example, a MIDI interface enables a computer to communicate with MIDI instruments and keyboards.

I/O
The part of a system that handles inputs and outputs, usually in the digital domain.

IPS
Inches Per Second. Used to describe tape speed.

IRQ
Interrupt Request. Part of the operating system of a computer that allows a connected device to request attention from the processor in order to transfer data to it or from it.

isopropyl alcohol
Type of alcohol commonly used for cleaning and de-greasing tape machine heads and guides.

jack plug
Commonly-used audio connector. May be mono (TS) or stereo (TRS).

jargon
Specialised words associated with a specialist subject.

k
Abbreviation for 1000 (kilo). Used as a prefix to other values to

indicate magnitude.

kHz
1000Hz.

kohm
1000 ohms.

LCD
Liquid crystal display.

LED
Light-Emitting Diode. Type of solid-state lamp.

limiter
Device that controls the gain of a signal so as to prevent it from ever exceeding a preset level. A limiter is essentially a fast-acting compressor with an infinite compression ratio.

linear
Device where the output is a direct multiple of the input.

line level
Mixers and signal processors tend to work at a standard signal level known as line level. In practice there are several different standard line levels, but all are in the order of a few volts. A nominal signal level is around -10dBv for semi-pro equipment and +4dBv for professional equipment.

load
Electrical circuit that draws power from another circuit or power supply. Also describes reading data into a computer.

load on/off
Function to allow the keyboard and sound-generating section of a keyboard synthesiser to be used independently of each other.

logic
Type of electronic circuitry used for processing binary signals comprising two discrete voltage levels.

loop
Circuit where the output is connected back to the input.

low-frequency oscillator (LFO)
Oscillator used as a modulation source, usually below 20Hz. The most common LFO waveshape is the sine wave, though there is often a choice of sine, square, triangular and sawtooth waveforms.

low-pass filter (LPF)
A filter which attenuates frequencies above its cutoff frequency.

LSB
Least Significant Byte. If a piece of data has to be conveyed as two bytes, one byte represents high-value numbers and the other low-value numbers, in much the same way as tens and units function in the decimal system. The high value, or most significant part of the message, is called the Most Significant Byte or MSB.

mA
Milliamp, or one thousandth of an amp.

MDM

Modular Digital Multitrack. A digital recorder that can be used in multiples to provide a greater number of synchronised tracks than a single machine.

M

Abbreviation for 1000,000, pronounced 'meg'. Examples are MHz, Mohm and so on.

memory

Computer's RAM memory used to store programs and data. This data is lost when the computer is switched off and so must be stored to disk or other suitable media.

menu

List of choices presented by a computer program or a device with a display window.

metal

Type of tape formulation capable of producing very high-quality recordings. Metal tape can only be used in specifically-designed machines.

mic level

Low-level signal generated by a microphone. This must be amplified many times to increase it to line level.

microprocessor

Specialised microchip at the heart of a computer. It is here that instructions are read and acted upon.

MIDI

Musical Instrument Digital Interface.

MIDI analyser
Device that gives a visual readout of MIDI activity when connected between two pieces of MIDI equipment.

MIDI bank change
Type of controller message used to select alternate banks of MIDI programs where access to more than 128 programs is required.

MIDI controller
Term used to describe the physical interface by means of which the musician plays the MIDI synthesiser or other sound generator. Examples of controllers are keyboards, drum pads, wind synths and so on.

MIDI control change
Also known as MIDI Controllers or Controller Data. These messages convey positional information relating to performance controls such as wheels, pedals, switches and other devices. This information can be used to control functions such as vibrato depth, brightness, portamento, effects levels, and many other parameters.

(standard) MIDI file
Standard file format for storing song data recorded on a MIDI sequencer in such as way as to allow it to be read by other makes or models of MIDI sequencer.

MIDI implementation chart
A chart, usually found in MIDI product manuals, which provides information as to which MIDI features are supported.

Supported features are marked with a 0 while unsupported feature are marked with a X. Additional information may be provided, such as the exact form of the bank change message.

MIDI in
The socket used to receive information from a master controller or from the MIDI Thru socket of a slave unit.

MIDI merge
Device or sequencer function that enables two or more streams of MIDI data to be combined.

MIDI mode
MIDI information can be interpreted by the receiving MIDI instrument in a number of ways, the most common being polyphonically on a single MIDI channel (poly-omni off mode). Omni mode enables a MIDI Instrument to play all incoming data regardless of channel.

MIDI module
Sound-generating device with no integral keyboard.

MIDI note number
Every key on a MIDI keyboard has its own note number, ranging from 0 to 127, where 60 represents middle C. Some systems use C3 as middle C while others use C4.

MIDI note off
MIDI message sent when key is released.

MIDI note on
Message sent when note is pressed.

MIDI out

MIDI connector used to send data from a master device to the MIDI In of a connected slave device.

MIDI port

MIDI connections of a MIDI-compatible device. A multiport, in the context of a MIDI interface, is a device with multiple MIDI output sockets, each capable of carrying data relating to a different set of 16 MIDI channels. Multiports are the only means of exceeding the limitations imposed by 16 MIDI channels.

MIDI program change

Type of MIDI message used to change sound patches on a remote module or the effects patch on a MIDI effects unit.

MIDI splitter

Alternative term for MIDI thru box.

MIDI sync

Description of the synchronisation systems available to MIDI users: MIDI Clock and MIDI Time Code.

MIDI thru

Socket on a slave unit used to feed the MIDI In socket of the next unit in line.

MIDI thru box

Device which splits the MIDI Out signal of a master instrument or sequencer to avoid daisy chaining. Powered circuitry is used to 'buffer' the outputs so as to prevent problems when many pieces of equipment are driven from a single MIDI output.

mixer

Device for combining two or more audio signals.

mixer ratios

If you see a mixer described as a 24:8:24:2, the first number is the number of input channels. The second number, in this case eight, means that the mixer has eight output groups. The third number tells us how many monitor channels the desk has, and if it's an in-line desk this will be the same as the number of input channels. If, on the other hand, it is a split console, the number of monitor channels may well be less than the number of input channels. Finally, the number two indicates that the main output of the desk is stereo.

monitor

Reference loudspeaker used for mixing.

monitoring

Action of listening to a mix or a specific audio signal.

mono

Single channel of audio information for reproduction over a single speaker. If multiple speakers are used, they all carry exactly the same signal.

MTC

MIDI Time Code, a MIDI equivalent of SMPTE time code using the same time and frame parameters. Unlike SMPTE, MTC is incorporated into the MIDI data stream and can be passed down the same cable as other MIDI data.

multisample

Creation of several samples, each covering a limited musical range, the idea being to produce a more natural range of sounds across the range of the instrument being sampled. For example, a piano may need to be sampled every two or three semitones in order to sound convincing.

multitimbral module

MIDI sound source capable of producing several different sounds at the same time and controlled on different MIDI channels.

multitrack

The process of recording a piece of music on a multitrack recording device so that different parts may be recorded at different times.

multitracker

Single piece of equipment which combines a multitrack tape recorder with a mixer. When spelled with a capital M, the term is a registered trademark of Fostex. The term Portastudio is also used generically by some people, but this is actually a trademark of the TEAC corporation. To my knowledge, there is no widely-used generic term for a cassette multitracker that doesn't rely on one or other of these brand names.

mute

Most studio mixers have Mute buttons on their input channels that turn off both the channel signal and any post-fade aux (effects) sends. Pre-fade (foldback) sends are not usually affected.

near field

Some people prefer the term 'close field' to describe a loudspeaker system designed to be used close to the listener. The advantage is that the listener hears more of the direct sound from the speakers and less of the reflected sound from the room.

noise gate
See Gate.

(tape) noise reduction
Systems such as Dolby or dbx are specific examples of encode/decode noise reduction systems inasmuch as they process the signal during recording and then apply the opposite process on playback. The processing is designed to bring about a decrease in tape hiss, though it doesn't affect any hiss that may have been recorded as part of the original signal.

noise shaping
System for creating digital dither so that any added noise is shifted into those parts of the audio spectrum where the human ear is least sensitive.

non-linear recording
Describes digital recording systems that allow any parts of the recording to be played back in any order with no gaps. Conventional tape is referred to as linear, because the material can only play back in the order in which it was recorded.

octave
A range of frequencies where the upper limit is twice the lower frequency.

off-line

Process carried out while a recording is not playing. For example, some computer-based processes have to be carried out off-line as the computer isn't fast enough to carry out the process in real time.

ohm

Unit of electrical resistance.

Ohm's law

Formula relating resistance, voltage and current in a resistive circuit: I=V/R where I is the current in amps, V is the voltage and R is resistance in ohms.

omni

Refers to a microphone that is equally sensitive in all directions, or to the MIDI mode in which data on all channels is recognised.

open circuit

Break in an electrical circuit that prevents current from flowing.

open reel

Tape machine on which the tape is wound on spools rather than sealed in a cassette.

oscillator

Circuit designed to generate a periodic electrical waveform.

overdub

To add another part to a multitrack recording or to replace one of the existing parts (see Dubbing).

overload
To exceed the operating capacity of an electronic or electrical circuit.

pad
Resistive circuit for reducing signal level.

pan pot
Control enabling the user of a mixer to move the signal to any point in the stereo soundstage by varying the relative levels fed to the left and right stereo outputs.

parallel
Method of connecting two or more circuits together so that their inputs and outputs are all connected together.

parameter
Variable value that affects some aspect of a device's performance.

passive
An electrical circuit that contains no active (amplifying) components. For example, a resistive pad is a passive circuit.

patch
Alternative term for program. Referring to a single programmed sound within a synthesiser that can be called up using program-change commands. MIDI effects units and samplers also have patches.

patch bay

System of panel-mounted connectors used to bring inputs and outputs to a central point from where they can be routed using plug-in patch cords.

patch cord

Short cable used with patch bays.

peak

Maximum instantaneous level of a signal.

PFL and solo

PFL (Pre-Fade Listen) is a system that allows any selected channel or aux send/return to be heard in isolation over the studio monitors. Because PFL is pre-fade (monitored prior to the channel fader), the level is independent of the position of the channel fader. When a channel's PFL button is pressed, all of the other channels (on which the PFL has not been pressed) are excluded from the monitor mix and, at the same time, the signal level of the channel you are checking is displayed on one of the console's meters. PFL is generally used in this way to set up the individual channel input gain trims.

phantom power

48v DC supply for capacitor microphones, transmitted along the signal cores of a balanced mic cable.

phase

Timing difference between two electrical waveforms expressed in degrees where 360° corresponds to a delay of exactly one cycle.

phase shift

Change of phase in a signal relative to its original form via time delay or other electrical/electronic processing.

phasing
Studio effect created by adding a phase-shifted signal to a non-phase-shifted signal and then varying the amount of phase shift.

phono plug
Hi-fi connector developed by RCA and used extensively on semi-pro, unbalanced recording equipment.

pitch
Musical interpretation of an audio frequency.

pitch bend
Special control message specifically designed to produce a change in pitch in response to the movement of a pitch bend wheel or lever. Pitch bend data can be recorded and edited, just like any other MIDI controller data, even though it isn't part of the controller message group.

pitch shifter
Device for changing the pitch of an audio signal without changing its duration.

polyphony
An instrument's ability to play two or more notes simultaneously. An instrument which can play only one note at a time is described as monophonic.

port
Connection for the input or output of data.

post-fade

Aux signal taken from after the channel fader so that the aux send level follows any channel fader changes. Normally used for feeding effects devices.

PPM

Peak Programme Meter. A meter designed to register signal peaks rather than the average level.

PPQN

Pulsed Per Quarter Note. Used in the context of MIDI clock-derived sync signals.

PQ coding

Process for adding pause, cue and other subcode information to a digital master tape in preparation for CD manufacture.

pre-fade

Aux signal taken from before the channel fader so that the channel fader has no effect on the aux send level. Normally used for creating foldback or cue mixes.

preset

Effects unit or synth patch that cannot be altered by the user.

pressure

Alternative term for aftertouch.

processor

Device designed to treat an audio signal by changing its dynamics or frequency content. Examples of processors include compressors, gates and equalisers.

program change

MIDI message designed to change instrument or effects unit patches.

pulse wave

Similar to a square wave but non-symmetrical. Pulse waves sound brighter and thinner than square waves, which means that they are useful in the synthesis of reed instruments. The timbre changes according to the mark/space ratio of the waveform.

pulse-width modulation

Means of modulating the duty cycle (mark/space ratio) of a pulse wave. This changes the timbre of the basic tone. LFO modulation of pulse width can be used to produce a pseudo-chorus effect.

punch in

Action of placing an already recorded track into record at the correct time during playback so that the existing material may be extended or replaced.

punch out

Action of switching a tape machine (or other recording device) out of record after executing a punch in. With most multitrack machines, both punching in and punching out can be accomplished without stopping the tape.

PZM

Pressure Zone Microphone. A type of boundary microphone, designed to reject out-of-phase sounds reflected from surfaces within the recording environment.

Q
Measurement of the resonant properties of a filter. The higher the Q, the more resonant the filter and the narrower the range of frequencies that are allowed to pass.

quantising
Means of moving notes recorded in a MIDI sequencer so that they line up with user defined subdivisions of a musical bar – 16s, for example. It may be used to correct timing errors, but over-quantising can remove the human feel from a performance.

RAM
Abbreviation for Random Access Memory, a type of memory used by computers for the temporary storage of programs and data. All data is lost when the power is turned off, and for that reason work needs to be saved to disk if it is not to be lost.

R-DAT
Rotary head Digital Audio Tape machine.

real time
Audio process that can be carried out as the signal is being recorded or played back. The opposite is off-line, where the signal is processed in non-real time.

release
Time taken for a level or gain to return to normal. Often used to describe the rate at which a synthesised sound reduces in level after a key has been released.

resistance
Opposition to the flow of electrical current. Measured in ohms.

resolution

Accuracy with which an analogue signal is represented by a digitising system. The more bits are used, the more accurately the amplitude of each sample can be measured, but there are other elements of converter design that also affect accuracy. High conversion accuracy is known as high resolution.

resonance

The degree to which a filter circuit or mechanical resonator emphasises a particular frequency. See Q.

reverb

Acoustic ambience created by multiple reflections in a confined space.

RF

Radio Frequency.

RF interference

Interference significantly above the range of human hearing.

ribbon microphone

Microphone in which the sound-capturing element is a thin metal ribbon suspended in a magnetic filed. When sound causes the ribbon to vibrate, a small electrical current is generated within the ribbon.

release

Rate at which a signal amplitude decays once a key has been released.

resonance

Characteristic of a filter that allows it to selectively pass a narrow range of frequencies (see Q).

RMS

Root Mean Square. A method of specifying the behaviour of a piece of electrical equipment under continuous sine wave testing conditions.

ROM

Abbreviation for Read-Only Memory. This is a permanent and non-volatile type of memory containing data that can't be changed. Operating systems are often stored on ROM as the memory remains intact when the power is switched off.

S/PDIF

Digital standard interfacing system for transferring stereo audio data from one piece of equipment to another. The connection format is an RCA phono connector, but specialised digital cable should be used.

sample

Process carried out by an A/D converter where the instantaneous amplitude of a signal is measured many times per second (44.1kHz in the case of CD).

sample

Digitised sound used as a musical sound source in a sampler or additive synthesiser.

sample rate

Number of times which an A/D converter samples the incoming waveform each second.

separation

Keeping sounds separate. In a studio where several musicians are playing together, each player's mic will tend to pick up some sound from the other instruments in the room. The lower the level of this unwanted spill the better the separation.

sequencer

Device for recording and replaying MIDI data, usually in a multitrack format, allowing complex compositions to be built up a part at a time.

short circuit

Low-resistance path that allows electrical current to flow. The term is usually used to describe a current path that exists through a faulty condition.

side chain

Part of a circuit that splits off a proportion of the main signal to be processed in some way. Compressors uses aside-chain signal to derive their control signals.

signal

Electrical representation of input such as sound.

signal chain

Route taken by a signal from the input of a system to its output.

signal-to-noise ratio

Ratio of maximum signal level to the residual noise, expressed in decibels.

sine wave
Waveform of a pure tone with no harmonics.

single-ended noise reduction
Device for removing or attenuating the noise component of a signal. Doesn't require previous coding, as with Dolby or dbx.

slave
Device under the control of a master device.

SMPTE
Time code developed for the film industry but now extensively used in music and recording. SMPTE is a real-time code and is related to hours, minutes, seconds and film or video frames rather than to musical tempo.

solo
Button on a mixer which isolates the channel in the monitor mix but, unlike PFL, the signal is post fader, which means that what you hear is the actual level of the signal in the mix. Most solo systems also retain the signal's pan position, which is why the term SIP (Solo In Place) is also commonly used. On a studio console, the main stereo output feeding the master stereo recorder is not interrupted when PFL, Solo or SIP are used.

spill
Term used to describe unwanted sound leaking into microphones. For example, in a live situation the drums and guitar amps will invariably spill into the vocal mics.

split
Means that the a mixer's monitor channels are physically

separate from the input channels and are probably located in the master section, to the right of the console.

standard MIDI file
Standard file format that allows MIDI files to be transferred between different sequencers and MIDI file players.

step time
System for programming a sequencer in non-real time.

stereo
Two-channel system feeding left and right loudspeakers in an attempt to recreate the way we perceive sounds coming from different directions.

stripe
To record time code onto one track of a multitrack tape machine.

subcode
Hidden data within the CD and DAT format that includes such information as the absolute time location, number of tracks, total running time and so on.

sustain
Part of the ADSR envelope which determines the level to which the sound will settle if a key is held down. Once the key is released, the sound decays at a rate set by the release parameter. Also refers to a guitar's ability to hold notes which decay very slowly.

sweet spot
Optimum position for a microphone or a listener relative to

monitor loudspeakers.

sync

Synchronisation, a process for making two or more time-dependent devices start together and run at exactly the same speed.

synthesiser

Electronic musical instrument designed to create a wide range of sounds, both imitative and abstract.

tape head

Part of a tape machine that transfers magnetic energy to the tape during recording or reads it during playback.

tempo

Rate of the beat of a piece of music, measured here in beats per minute.

thru

MIDI connector which passes on the signal received at the MIDI In socket. See MIDI thru.

track

Originally a tape-based term, track relates to the physical section of tape used to store individual parts of the recording. Tracks are parallel to each other and are recorded and played back using a multisection head so as to keep them separate until they are mixed. The term has now been carried over to digital tape and hard disk recording systems, though the term is mainly conceptual in this context inasmuch as the data is not recorded on individual, parallel tracks.

tracking

System whereby one device follows another. Tracking is often discussed in the context of MIDI guitar synthesisers or controllers where the MIDI output attempts to track the pitch of the guitar strings.

transparency

Subjective term used to describe audio quality where the high-frequency detail is clear and individual sounds are easy to identify and separate.

transpose

To shift a musical signal by a fixed number of semitones.

TRS jack

Stereo-type jack with tip, ring and sleeve connections.

unbalanced

Two-wire electrical signal connection where the inner (hot or positive) conductor is usually surrounded by the cold (negative) conductor, forming a screen against interference.

unison

Musical term relating to two or more instruments or sounds playing the same notes at the same time.

valve

Active circuit device involving a heated cathode, a grid and an anode sealed in an evacuated glass tube. Also known as a tube.

VCA

Voltage-Controlled Amplifier.

VCF
Voltage-Controlled Filter.

VCO
Voltage-Controlled Oscillator.

velocity
The rate at which a key is depressed. This may be used to control loudness (to simulate the response of instruments such as pianos) or other parameters on later synthesisers.

vibrato
Pitch modulation using a low-frequency oscillator to modulate a voltage-controlled oscillator.

voice
Capacity of a synthesiser to play a single musical note. An instrument capable of playing 16 simultaneous notes is said to be a 16-voice instrument.

volt
Unit of measurement of electrical potential energy.

VU meter
Meter designed to interpret signal levels in roughly the same way as the human ear, which responds more closely to the average levels of sounds rather than to the peak levels.

warmth
Subjective term used to describe sound where the bass and low mid frequencies have depth and where the high frequencies are smooth sounding rather than being aggressive

or fatiguing. Warm-sounding tube equipment may also exhibit some of the aspects of compression.

wah
Filter sweep effect, originally developed for use in guitar pedals.

watt
Unit of electrical power.

waveform
Graphic representation of the way in which a sound wave or electrical wave varies with time.

white noise
Random signal with an energy distribution that produces the same amount of noise power per Hz.

XLR
Type of connector commonly used to carry balanced audio signals, including the feeds from microphones.

Y-lead
Lead split so that one source can feed two destinations. Y-leads may also be used in console insert points, when a stereo jack plug at one end of the lead is split into two monos at the other.

zero crossing point
Point at which a signal waveform crosses from being positive to negative and vice versa.